Dr Krishna R. Dronamraju is a geneticist who received his training under J.B.S. Haldane. He is founder and president of the Foundation for Genetic Research in Houston. He is an Honorary Research Fellow of University College, London; an Invited Professor of the University of Paris; and a Visiting Professor of Osmania University, Hyderabad (India). He served as an Adviser to the White House and as a member of the U.S Government's Recombinant DNA Advisory Committee, National Institutes of Health. His primary research interests include human gene therapy and ethics of biotechnology sharing by the developing world.

His books include *Haldane* (a biography of J.B.S. Haldane), *The History and Development of Human Genetics*, *If I am To Be Remembered* (a biography of Sir Julian Huxley), and Haldane's *Daedalus Revisited*.

Biological and Social Issues in Biotechnology Sharing

KRISHNA R. DRONAMRAJU
*Foundation for Genetic Research,
Texas, USA*

LONDON AND NEW YORK

First published 1998 by Ashgate Publishing

Reissued 2018 by Routledge
2 Park Square, Milton Park, Abingdon, Oxon, OX14 4RN
711 Third Avenue, New York, NY 10017

Routledge is an imprint of the Taylor & Francis Group, an informa business

Copyright © Krishna R. Dronamraju 1998

All rights reserved. No part of this book may be reprinted or reproduced or utilised in any form or by any electronic, mechanical, or other means, now known or hereafter invented, including photocopying and recording, or in any information storage or retrieval system, without permission in writing from the publishers.

Notice:
Product or corporate names may be trademarks or registered trademarks, and are used only for identification and explanation without intent to infringe.

Publisher's Note
The publisher has gone to great lengths to ensure the quality of this reprint but points out that some imperfections in the original copies may be apparent.

Disclaimer
The publisher has made every effort to trace copyright holders and welcomes correspondence from those they have been unable to contact.

A Library of Congress record exists under LC control number: 98073402

ISBN 13: 978-1-138-61191-7 (hbk)
ISBN 13: 978-1-138-61195-5 (pbk)
ISBN 13: 978-0-429-46088-3 (ebk)

It gives me great pleasure to dedicate this book to my friend, Ambassador Roy Huffington

Contents

List of tables		viii
Foreword		x
1	Introduction	1
2	Biotechnology and society	7
3	Patenting culture in science	17
4	Patenting micro-organisms: the Chakrabarty case	23
5	Different types of biotechnological innovations	27
6	International treaties	37
7	Safety considerations for transgenic organisms	53
8	Intellectual property rights and plant genetic resources	65
9	Conservation of medicinal plants	79
10	Patenting cDNA sequences: the NIH controversy	101
11	NIH patent policy	115
12	Patenting human gene therapy	123
13	IPR in a north-south context	129
14	Is a uniform IPR system necessary?	139
15	Ethical issues in transfer of technology	149
Bibliography		157
Index		163

List of tables

Table	1.1	Classification of nations according to the strength of their intellectual property laws	3
Table	1.2	Countries signing science and technology agreements and IPR Annex with the U.S.	5
Table	6.1	Comparison of PBR under the UPOV Convention and Patent Law	44
Table	6.2	Number of threatened species	45
Table	6.3	Systems of biodiversity	45
Table	6.4	Number of recorded species that have been extinct since 1600	46
Table	6.5	International agreements	46
Table	6.6	Member countries, Budapest Treaty on the International Recognition of Micro-organisms for the Purposes of Patent Procedure	47
Table	6.7	Member countries, European Patent Convention	47
Table	6.8	Member countries, Paris Union Convention	48
Table	6.9	Member countries, Patent Cooperation Treaty (PCT)	50
Table	6.10	Member countries, Union for the Protection of New Varieties of Plants	51
Table	7.1	Field tests of genetically engineered crops in the U.S.A.	56
Table	7.2	Number and percentage of approvals of field trials of engineered plants by traits and by country	58
Table	7.3	Some examples of gene flow from crops to wild relatives resulting in new or worse weeds	59
Table	8.1	Human behavior and social changes affecting biological diversity	69
Table	8.2	Wildlife habitat loss by conversion: Asia and Africa	70
Table	8.3	Diminishing bird populations in Great Britain (1970-1988)	71
Table	8.4	Desertification of world's rangelands within the drylands (in thousands of hectares)	71

Table	8.5	PBR in five Latin American countries (1995)	77
Table	9.1	Domestic regulation and international competition	90
Table	9.2	World demand for prescription drugs (1980 estimates)	90
Table	9.3	Some commonly used medicinal plants	91
Table	9.4	Medicinal exports of India	92
Table	9.5	Number of threatened species	100
Table	11.1	NIH foreign filing procedure for U.S. filed patent applications	118
Table	13.1	Countries at varying stages of scientific and technological development	132

Foreword

by M.S. SWAMINATHAN

Among the several spectacular scientific advances of this century, molecular mapping of chromosomes and genetic engineering occupy a prominent place. Biotechnology has started making a significant impact on medical and agricultural research. The enormous power conferred by molecular genetics on the human ability to manipulate living organisms has raised serious questions of ethics and equity. The basic feedstock for the biotechnology industry is biodiversity. Countries rich in biodiversity, mostly occurring in the developing world, often lack biotechnological capability. In contrast, industrialised countries, though poor in endemic biodiversity, have considerable genetic engineering skills. They are increasingly getting all their findings protected under IPR regulations.

Thus, we witness a growing paradox. The rural and tribal families of the developing world, who are conserving biodiversity at personal cost for national and international public good, remain poor, while those who utilise their material and knowledge in molecular and Mendelian breeding become rich. It is to end this unethical situation that the legally binding global Convention on Biological Diversity (CBD) has provisions which integrate equity in benefit sharing with the sustainable use of genetic resources. India is proposing to introduce legislation which will accord recognition and reward to both the breeder and the primary conservers.

In 1999, the provisions of TRIPS (Trade Related Intellectual Property Rights) of the World Trade Agreement will be due for review. It will be important that this occasion is utilized for integrating the provisions of CBD relating to equity and ethics with those of conventional IPR regulations.

Prof Krishna Dronamraju is to be congratulated for writing this timely and incisive book. This book will be of great value to those interested in IPR issues and will help the international community to develop and adopt a new TRIPS regime which is rooted not only in the principles of economics, but also of ecology, ethics and equity. We owe Prof Dronamraju a deep sense of gratitude for this labour of love in the cause of science for human welfare.

1 Introduction

There is hardly any one among the educated public who is not familiar with Intellectual Property Rights (IPR) although the full meaning of these words may not always be clearly understood. Intellectual property mainly consists of patents, copyrights, trademarks, trade secrets, and plant breeder's rights. The primary purpose of promoting IPR is to provide an incentive for creating new inventions, especially by individual inventors. Patents are also viewed as major incentives for large firms to encourage inventiveness and invest a significant share of the profits in R & D. Some believe that patents also help in disseminating information about new inventions sooner than later. On the other hand, others believe that patents tend to hinder rather than encourage R & D by maintaining secrecy and by blocking free access to information. There is also the widespread belief in the developing countries that the IPR systems are mainly designed by the developed nations for the specific purpose of exploiting the natural resources of developing countries. Furthermore, creation of monopoly positions by large firms in selected industries increases the social costs. Ideally, a nation's patent laws must reflect a balancing of incentives for inventors and rapid diffusion of new technology (Mansfield, 1993).

Most books on the subject of IPR are either written or edited by lawyers. Quite understandably, they have tended to examine the legal issues involved. As a geneticist and biologist, with a background in human genetics, I am primarily interested in the nature of patents in biotechnology, their ethical and social implications, and the impact of patents on the biodiversity of our planet. Also, one born in India, a developing nation, I am deeply interested in the IPR systems of developing countries and their impact on the trade relations between developing and developed nations. Several pages are devoted to this particular aspect.

One of the most controversial aspects of this subject is the discussion surrounding the whole issue of patenting human genes. The pros and cons of this debate and the ethical and social issues involved are of great interest. Another aspect of IPR which has aroused deep passions in the developing world is the protection of plant genetic resources including both food crops and medicinal plants. Plant breeder's rights have received special attention in India in recent years, partly due to the efforts of Professor M.S. Swaminathan of Madras. This has led to the first legislation proposed to the Indian Parliament to protect plant breeder's rights.

It is hoped that this book will help to stimulate further interest in the subject of IPR, creating a realistic understanding of the controversial issues involved. It is a subject which is becoming increasingly important as more and more research is being privatized. Because of budgetary constraints, many universities are entering into contracts with private industries to market their inventions. Increasing research collaboration between academia, business, and government is leading to a greater awareness of the importance of IPR systems.

Future developments will show whether IPR systems will prove to be a stimulus for increasing R & D or a hindrance to free exchange of information. It also remains to be seen if IPR will serve to protect biodiversity or merely serve to exploit and deplete world's natural resources. The answer to these questions largely depends on what kind of IPR we are likely to develop globally and whether a meaningful dialogue can occur between the developed and developing nations.

Developing nations may eventually develop their own special brand of IPR which would suit their economic interests better than the western models. As Evenson (1993) aptly put it: "As developing countries recover from the 'surprise attack' launched by the United States and converted into the GATT initiative, they may be able to develop a more positive set of tactics and programs than they have managed to date. For the short run, they could bargain aggressively with the developed countries for trade concessions, in return for strengthened domestic treatment of foreigners' intellectual property. Developing countries have not been very good at this. Their stance has been one of continued resistance to strengthening IPRs and including them in the GATT. They would probably do better by acknowledging that IPRs are going to be part of trade laws and policy, and then proceeding to bargain for concessions".

Whatever direction the present negotiations may lead to, IPR issues are here to stay for good or evil and they are expected to play an increasingly important role in international relations. It is also correct to say that IPR have been around, in one form or another, from the dawn of civilization, and have played a significant role in promoting international trade and commerce.

This book is intended for educated lay readers as well as individuals in the legal, scientific, medical or business professions who may wish to know more about the issues surrounding the IPR systems. It can also be used in teaching courses in these professions at the graduate or undergraduate levels.

Pamela Smith (1996), in a review of global intellectual property rights, classified various nations according to the strength of their intellectual property laws (as compared to the IPR standards proposed by the U.S. Chamber of Commerce) – see Tables 1.1 and 1.2.

Table 1.1 Classification of nations according to the strength of their intellectual property laws

Meet the minimum standard	Fiji	Tanzania
	Finland	Trinidad and
Belgium	ghana	Tobago
Cyprus	Greece	Uganda
Denmark	Grenada	Vanuatu
France	Guinea	Western Samoa
Germany	Guyana	Zimbabwe
Israel	Iceland	
Italy	Ireland	**Flaws in laws and some**
Luxembourg	Japan	**enforcement**
Netherlands	Jordan	
Republic of	Malawi	Armenia
South Africa	Malta and Gozo	Azerbaijan
Sweden	Mauritius	Barbados
Switzerland	Morocco	Belarus
United Kingdom	New Zealand	Costa Rica
United States	Nigeria	Czechoslovakia
	Norway	Dominica
Generally good laws	Philippines	El Salvador
	Rwanda	Estonia
Antigua	Sierra Leone	Georgia
Australia	Singapore	
Austria	Soloman Islands	
Bahamas	Spain	
Bahrain	Sri Lanka	
Belize	St. Lucia	
Botswana	St. Vincent	
Burundi	Sudan	
Canada	Swaziland	

Table 1.1   Classification of nations according to the strength of their intellectual property laws (continued)

Flaws in laws and some enforcement (cont'd)	Cameroon	Brazil
	Central African Republic	China
Guatemala	Chad	Ecuador
Haiti	Chile	Honduras
Hungary	Colombia	India
Jamaica	Congo	Paraguay
Kazakhstan	Dominican Republic	Peru
Latvia	Egypt	Thailand
Lesotho	Gabon	The Gambia
Lithuania	Iran	Turkey
Malaysia	Ivory Coast	Yemen Arab
Moldova	Kusait	Republic
Nepal	Mali	
Pakistan	Mauritania	**No IPR laws**
Portugal	Mexico	
Russia	Nicaragua	Comoros
Saudi Arabia	Niger	Equatorial Guinea
Tajikistan	Panama	Ethiopia
Tunisia	Poland	Guinea-Bissau
Turkmenistan	Romania	Indonesia
Ukraine	Senegal	Laos
Uruguay	Slovenia	Madagascar
Uzbekistan	Syrian Arab	Maldive Islands
Zambia	Republic	Mozambique
	togo	Oman
Seriously flawed laws	Venezuela	Papua New Guinea
		Qatar
Algeria	**Inadequate protection laws**	Suriname
Bangladesh		Tongo
Benin		United Arab Republic
Bulgaria	Argentina	
Burkina	Bolivia	

Source: *Science Communication*, vol. 17, 357-378, 1996.

Table 1.2 Countries signing science and technology agreements and an IPR Annex with the U.S.

Belarus
Brazil
Chile
China
Czech Republic
Finland
Hungary
Indonesia
Italy
Japan
Kazakhstan
Korea
Republic of Poland
Russia
Republic of Slovenia
Slovak Republic
Ukraine
Venezuela

2 Biotechnology and society

Public perception of biotechnology is influenced by several factors:

Financial success The commercial success of biotechnology is a well known phenomenon in recent years. Market research in the U.S. has shown that human health care was the focus of research for most companies, whereas agriculture and chemicals were the focus of far fewer firms. Environmental applications of biotechnology were even less represented. For pharmaceutical companies the percentage of price change in stock performance in a recent year ranged from 35 percent to 160 percent. For agricultural biotechnology companies, the range of increase during the same period was 11 percent to 103 percent. A big share of the basic research which led to biotechnology in the U.S. today was funded by the National Institutes of Health. The industry thus created had annual revenues of $ 4 billion in 1991-92. It is estimated further that the two areas of greatest impact–health and agriculture– account for more than $ 1 trillion value in goods and services.

Media coverage Frequent media coverage through television, newspapers and magazines has heightened public awareness of biotechnology. Awareness and appreciation of biotechnology is further heightened by sensational events such as a new discovery which could lead to a cure for cancer or the award of Nobel prizes for certain achievements. Occasionally, negative publicity also results from perceived evils of technology such as the possible toxic effects of human gene therapy or the impact of "transgenes" on various farm animals and crops. The adverse impact of technology on ecology was heightened by the oil spill from Exxon Valdez in Alaska although that situation did not directly involve biotechnology. But in the public mind such subtle distinctions may not seem particularly significant.

Crisis An occasional crisis may lead to greater attention on biotechnology. Examples are the high cost of certain therapeutic drugs and other substances (e.g.

insulin) or the shortage of blood, both leading to research to discover artificial substitutes.

Apprehension   Paradoxically, attempts to regulate biotechnology lead to greater apprehension among the public. Appropriate regulation that is justified on scientific grounds should be encouraged. Excessive zeal in regulating biotechnology would tend to discourage the growth of biotechnology industry.

Biotechnology

What is biotechnology? It may be simply defined as the application of biological knowledge for the purpose of solving practical problems in heathcare, agriculture, and related fields. It encompasses a whole range of problems in food production and nutrition, hygiene and public health, to name a few of the many areas of technology it covers.

In what follows, I propose to consider certain aspects of human genetics and agriculture and draw some general observations concerning the transfer of biotechnology to the developing nations and intellectual property rights.

Human genetics

The genetic burden of the population is expressed in the appearance of various congenital malformations and diseases. In some instances these diseases have a late age of onset. In other cases, the genetic burden is expressed in terms of varying degrees of fetal mortality. The cumulative effect can be measured in terms of "Darwinian" fitness, namely the impairment of reproductive capacity as a result of the underlying genetic burden.

In recent years, the traditional pedigree studies have been replaced by "reverse" genetics. That is to say, the recombinant DNA techniques have made it possible to locate the gene on a specific segment of the chromosome first, and later the gene sequence and the protein product are studied. In classical genetics, the chromosomal location is the eventual goal, not the beginning.

Human gene therapy is being attempted now on a limited scale but only for somatic cells, not for gonodal cells. Consequently, our present experience is limited to immediate somatic cell therapy which has no bearing on subsequent generations.

In the U.S., this is carefully regulated by the National Institutes of Health and its "Recombinant DNA Advisory Committee" of which I am a member. The technique of gene therapy generally includes the introduction of a new sequence or a rearranged piece of DNA (which is usually derived from the patient's DNA itself) into the diseased cells of the patient, for instance the tumor cells in certain cancers. In other instances, the transfer is achieved with known markers for the purpose of improving techniques of "transfection", but may not involve any gene transfer.

Human gene therapy is still very much in its infancy. Several scientists as well as the lay public have voiced much concern about its possible adverse effects. However, only somatic cell therapy has been attempted so far. The possibility of germ line therapy, which could alter the composition of the future gene pool, is still being debated. In order to address the concerns regarding the possibility of toxicity and to ensure that the required results are obtained, the following aspects should be considered in planning somatic cell therapy: (a) the availability of an adequate source of the correct gene, (b) single or fewer treatments of "gene therapy" must by involved, (c) there must be a high efficiency delivery system to reach the target cell, (d) minimal toxic effects, (e) adjacent cells unaffected, (f) possible to regulate the introduced gene product, (h) therapy must be performed before irreversible pathology occurs, and (i) benefits must outweigh the risks.

Patentability?

What is patentable in human genetics? Naturally occurring gene sequences are certainly *not* patentable, either from a moral or legal point of view. Laboratory techniques of novel DNA analysis and methods leading to certain "valuable" sequences may be patentable depending upon the circumstances, the products of gene technology may be patentable, and certain techniques of "gene therapy" may be patentable. This is a rapidly evolving field and new techniques of treating various types of cancer may be patented in the near future.

However, much of the recombinant DNA technology as applied to human genetics is beyond the capacity of almost all developing nations at present. Consequently, any concern regarding the possibility of illegal copying of these techniques or processes is not warranted at the present time.

Agriculture

In agriculture, both techniques and products have been identified for the purpose of patenting long before the developments in human genetics. However, recombinant DNA technology has introduced new methods and new products, for instance, the role of "transgenes" in creating new varieties, and these new developments have complicated the process of patenting.

Several problems of patenting and transfer of biotechnology to the developing nations have been identified before (see Swaminathan and Jana, 1992). Some are listed here: (a) there is the problem of non-recognition of certain traditional practices of culling and selections under the modern context of "intellectual property rights", (b) the basic incompatibility between introduction of new biotechnologies and conservation of genetic diversity, for instance, a new recombinant strain of wheat may be replacing several previously existing local strains, (c) the ecological impact of the introduction of new plant varieties and new genotypes, (d) the drain of precious rare species and resources from the developing nations, mainly due to the loss of their habitat because of rapid population growth. Certain other concerns are discussed below.

Intellectual property rights

In general, the incentive for patenting a certain idea, method, or product is to protect its unfair use by others without benefit to its inventor. However, different nations have different regulations and national standards regarding intellectual property rights (IPR). Consequently, only well regulated international agreements can monitor the observance or violation of patent regulations.

Patenting itself is a long and laborious process. In the U.S., the average time for obtaining a patent is 21 months whereas in Japan the corresponding period is three years. There are also great differences in the degree of sensitivity to the patenting of micro-organisms and biological tissues. For instance, it is only since 1987 that Taiwan's patent law has been amended to include pharmaceuticals and chemicals. Also, each country may excel in a particular type of industry or technology. The fermentation industry is strong in South Korea but there is a shortage of trained manpower. Indeed, this is a common problem in many developing nations. Trained manpower, especially trained managers and leaders in biotechnology are lacking in most developing nations. Hence, several of these nations have not been able to develop a sophisticated understanding of the subtlety of the legal and other aspects of the patenting of biological tissues and processes.

Constraints on acceptance of new technologies

For several reasons the acceptance of new technologies including biotechnology is a slow process in the developing nations. There are different levels of sophistication in the developing nations. Any transfer of biotechnology will have to take into account the degree of compatibility between the two nations. This includes a recognition of levels of technology, economy, technical manpower, and national needs.

Transfer of biotechnology should not be a prelude to economic or technological imperialism. The purpose of such transfer should be of benefit to both the nations. In particular, it should contribute to the acceleration of development of the developing nation.

The above discussion can be summarized as follows:
- (a) lack of familiarity of new technologies,
- (b) financial concerns about the cost of adopting the new technology,
- (c) lack of trained leaders and technical manpower,
- (d) lack of facilities to monitor or safeguard against possible toxic effects. However, a recent white paper on "Rice Biosafety" stated that progress has been made in many Asian countries to develop regulatory systems governing the importation, testing, commercialization, and export of transgenic plants, including rice (Clegg et al, 1993),
- (e) fear of economic exploitation,
- (f) fear of loss of raw materials and natural resources,
- (g) lack of sensitivity for patenting biological tissues and micro-organisms,
- (h) concern about non-recognition of indigenous practices and traditional methods,
- (i) potential incompatibility between new biotechnologies and conservation of naturally occurring genetic diversity,
- (j) fear of biological and chemical contamination,
- (k) lack of public awareness and political support.

Biotechnology as a part of social milieu

The development of any technology is an integral part of the socio-political milieu of that particular nation. This applies both to nations which supply the technology as well as the recipient nations. Beyond the technical and financial concerns lie several political and social factors which ultimately define the successful acceptance of any new technology. Such social factors as public health and hygiene, energy resources, food production, transportation, communications and electronics as well as traditional religious beliefs and attitudes can impact on the acceptance and development of new technologies.

Science, technology and ethics

Many years ago, J.B.S. Haldane, in his book *Daedalus or Science and the Future* (1923), urged that unless our ethical outlook evolves to keep pace with the development of science and technology, social chaos and disaster would result. Haldane's prediction seems even more valid today. In a reprint of *Daedalus*, several leading scientists support this point of view (Dronamraju, 1995). Haldane argued that any religion which would satisfy the scientific point of view must recognize the provisional nature of ethics. Ethics are bound by time, culture and knowledge. Transfer of new technologies invariably complicates the existing state of ethics. It introduces questions which did not exist prior to its transfer. Therein lies the problem.

Transfer of technology, especially biotechnology, imposes ethical dilemmas for both exporting and receiving nations. Are we limiting the options for the next generation? Such "trans-national" and "trans-generational" technological imperialism poses grave dangers for the future. Paradoxically, this situation results from a desire on the part of the developing nations to achieve economic independence. Many developing nations seem to adopt an indiscriminate policy towards the adoption of new technologies without any regard to its impact on future generations. One great concern is its impact on ecology. Another is its impact on public health. Surely, the experience of developed nations can help developing nations that intend to follow a similar path.

One can recognize at least three fundamental types of ethical conflicts:
    (a) ethical dilemmas in the developed nations in relation to the export of new technologies,

(b) ethical dilemmas in the developing nations in relation to technology and economic priorities, and
(c) ethical dilemmas in the developing nations in relation to technology and political independence (self-reliance).

Unlimited and excessive zeal for adopting new technologies can easily play havoc with the development of developing nations. I have already mentioned some of these. The areas of concern include lack of leaders and facilities to screen for possible and technological dependence on foreign nations, upsetting a proper balance of priorities and national resources, and possible conflicts with existing cultural and religious beliefs and traditions. To mention a simple and obvious example, one is shocked by the fumes and suffocating pollution from motor vehicles that is evident during peak hours of traffic in New Delhi; there do not seem to be any emission controls or environmental quality standards. If this happens to be the situation in such a basic aspect of life as automobile emission, what can we say about the regulation of more complex aspects of technology? What about the testing of numerous pharmaceuticals and commercially available nutritional products? What about the control of factory emissions, especially sulfur dioxide and its related compounds? What about the contamination of soil and water as well as food crops, fruits, vegetables and milk by increasing quantities of pesticides? What is the impact of all these contaminants on the frequency of various types of cancers, congenital malformations and fetal mortality in the human populations? How many developing nations can afford to possess adequate facilities to monitor such concerns? The U.S. model is not particularly encouraging because safety concerns remain very high in spite of several existing regulatory agencies in the United States. The concern should be greater in the developing nations where no such facilities exist.

Science, technology and religion

Sir Peter Medawar (1984, p. 66) in his book, *The Limits of Science*, emphasized (the "ultimate questions" of Karl Popper) the limits of science. Science cannot (and is not designed to) answer such questions as:

      How did everything begin?
      What are we all here for?
      What is the point of living?

Nobel laureate Joshua Lederberg (1995) recently stated that "science is bereft of deontology". Science is not a substitute for religion. In matters of technology, one must maintain reasonable expectations in order to limit later disappointments and frustrations. Otherwise, a backlash against science and technology would be the result. Francis Bacon, in Book I of *De Dignitat et Augmentis Scientiarum*, expounded on the limitations of science. He mentioned three:

> The first, that we not so place our felicity in knowledge as we forget our mortality: the second, that we make application of knowledge to give ourselves repose and contentment and not distaste or repining: the third, that we do not presume by the contemplations of nature to attain the mysteries of God (Trans. Wats. 1674; reproduced from Medawar, 1984, pp. 65-66).

Unfortunately, science and technology have raised our expectations in what we are led to believe is their promise for the future. I refer to economic growth and better living standards which are expected to result from the application of modern technology. Consequently many in the developing world hope to achieve these goals by copying the technological and industrial methods of the western world. While there is no assurance that an equal success in living standards would be achieved in the developing world, it is almost certain that the acquisitions of new technologies tends to displace or transform traditional cultures and indigenous skills. This is mainly due to their economic inviability under the changed social circumstances. It is obvious that new technologies tend to damage the existing social fabric, and this change may not always be a desirable one.

Population explosion

It is well know that the population of the developing world is increasing at a much faster rate than that of the developed nations. It may not be meaningful to emulate an American of European model because the specific technological requirements and the anticipated rate of change would be quite different in these two situations. Any modest gains in living standards in India, for instance, are outstripped soon by the rapid increase in the population. This, in turn, sets in motion a complex spiral of interaction between technology, economy, unemployment, national resources and priorities.

Another important consequence of the application of technology is the creation of a new "caste" system based on the technological education and employment.

Ironically, adoption of new technologies tends to increase the divide between different groups within a nation (e.g. between the white and black populations in the United States). Developing nations which rapidly embrace new technologies may be creating similar divisions within their populations. It creates a job market which is beyond the aspirations of most young people who received traditional education. In other words, in order for a technology to be successfully adopted, a nation must have a continuous cycle of employment and training as well as a new type of education at all levels. Needless to say, many developing nations are not prepared to face such obligations. As a result of the raised expectations of their populations, social and political unrest and disorder would be the logical result of a poorly planned technological world.

Few would display the zeal and enthusiasm for scientific applications today as was the case with Haldane's (1923) *Daedalus*; perhaps not even Haldane! Haldane (1923) wrote as follows: "In general the effect of a religious morality is to hamstring man's moral development. The true path lay in the use of each difficulty as it arose as a stepping stone to the next stage of moral advance".

To conclude, successful transfer of biotechnology depends not only on economic and scientific considerations but also on the level of public perception within the socio-political, religious, moral and ethical context of that particular community.

3 Patenting culture in science

Recent years have seen the emergence of a patent culture in public sector science, especially the growing commercialization at the intersection of university and government-sponsored research on the one hand and private industry on the other. Some have viewed this trend with great apprehension because the growing commercialization of science is believed to be a threat to the long-established conventions and norms of public sector, especially university research (for instance, see Bozeman and Crow, 1991). A common fear is that the profit motive–the cornerstone of commercialization–would undermine the normal implication of the patent culture for the way scientific work is recognized and rewarded, the process by which the credibility of science is protected. Both scientific work and patents depend on the dissemination and evaluation of knowledge. A patent may be regarded as yet another form of scientific claim. Each brings its own rewards. This subject was recently reviewed by Packer and Webster (1996). Narin (1994) has suggested that, for bibliometric purposes, patents and papers may be treated much the same way. A patent can be regarded as yet another form of scientific claim.

Competence and novelty

Packer and Webster (1996) evaluated the culture of patenting in British universities. Among those surveyed, the response rate was 44.0 percent, but there was much variation among them. The number of patents studied was 572. While some universities had none, one held about 60 patents. Thirty percent of the universities had no formal policy on intellectual property. Sixty percent of the respondents stated that patents were not self-financing. For further study, the investigators selected ten universities that had some patenting activity and two fields of research –pharmacology and biotechnology. These were selected because of their different patent histories and traditions; pharmacology is a well established field with a long history of well know patents and biotechnology is a relatively new field with a short patenting history. Of particular interest was the extent of connection, if any, these groups may have established with industry and a comparison of their research experiences with those of industrial scientists. The study also included five corporations in the pharmaceutical and biotechnology industries. The central theme of their research is the use and construction of concepts such as 'novelty' and 'scope', from both legal and technical points of view. Another important aspect of the study was the degree of "credibility" that may affect the practice of scientific research as well as the practice of the patenting process. Special attention was focused on two questions: how do scientists acquire patents, and what do scientists do with patents once they have been granted. Finally, how are scientific findings transformed into patents?

Two facts became obvious at once; the process of recognition by one's peers and the time required to convince others of one's claims can be quite lengthy. Financial costs needed to complete national and international patenting procedures are often too high to be affordable by an individual. These are usually met by a firm that had received licensing rights from a university.

Competencies required for successful patenting[1]

(modified after Packer and Webster, 1996; and Fujimura, 1997)

1. Production phase
   - understanding the legal implications

---

[1]Patenting process has also been discussed as a socio-cultural paradigm, a cultural infrastructure, which scientists need to understand thoroughly to be able to develop the technical and social skills needed for patenting. Fujimura's (1987) notions of "production" work and "articulation" work have been discussed by Packer and Webster (1996) in terms of sociotechnical competencies, with special reference to the intersection of science and the patenting process. According to Fujimura (1987), meeting the requirements of the patenting process requires changes in the experimental and social work of the laboratory. Scientists seeking to patent an invention must be able to provide a summary of the invention, evaluate that invention in the context of existing patents, perform the kind of research that would clinch a patent claim, and be able to arrange the publication date to match patenting needs. This may include postponing the date of publication or conducting further research to meet the patenting requirements.

- searching patent literature
- writing patent examples and formulating claims.
2. Articulation work
    - performing new experiments to embody a patent claim
    - planning research around existing patents
    - altering or delaying publication to avoid damaging patent application.

Novelty in science

Scientists should be able to recognize and distinguish between scientific and legal versions of the novelty of their work. Failure to recognize patentability on the part of industrial liaison personnel is often due to the lack of specialist and technical knowledge across a number of scientific disciplines. Two important requirements —novelty and nonobviousness—are perceived by the scientific community very differently from the way originality of academic work is judged. The legal concept of novelty of an invention requires that it must not have been publicly disclosed by the applicant or anyone else before the application has been filed (or one year prior to the filing in the United States). Disclosure includes any form of publication, presentation, commercial use, or any form of oral disclosure not covered by a confidentiality agreement. The requirement of nonobviousness is closely related to originality. The invention should not have been an *obvious* extension of the existing knowledge or practice (*prior art*), yet others should be able to repeat a procedure or produce a specific product by following the information that is provided in the patent application. Furthermore, as emphasized by Packer and Webster (1996), a patent examiners' decision should be based on what prior art was available at the time of filing, even though several months or years may have elapsed since the initial application had been filed.

The British scientists, who participated in the study conducted by Packer and Webster (1996), saw scientific advance in small gradual steps, not in grandiose terms of intellectual history. However, most of them recognized the difference between the two kinds of novelty—one in terms of academic science and the other in terms of the legal definition of patentability. I have previously discussed the slow progress of science in terms of small gradual steps, under the heading of "intellectual hybridization", which often involves the creation of new fields of science by synthesizing diverse concepts in existing disciplines (Dronamraju,

1989). This process is contrary to the view that science progresses by means of abrupt revolutions, as defined by Kuhn (1962). The gradual process of scientific progress in terms of small steps obviously complicates the ease with which one can claim patentability of ideas and inventions in science. In some instances, what is obviously regarded as a novelty in scientific research, may not be patentable at all.[2]

There had been a widespread misconception that patents are only concerned with major advances in science, although it is now increasingly realized that the patent system generally deals with incremental changes. Quite often, scientists are surprised how trivial a patentable subject appears to be from an academic research point of view. In the British survey, one scientist felt some embarrassment at being named an inventor that the scientist regarded as obvious: "I am in a bit of an awkward position because I suggested that they do it, but it is so obvious from the literature and it is so derivative that I am absolutely surprised that it issued". Another scientist stated that the main reason for not proceeding with the patent application was because of the difficulty in deciding whether what he would report would be regarded as new from a scientific point of view. On the other hand, those who believed that patenting requires less originality from the scientist also found it more difficult to present their work as a patentable invention. These difficulties make it clear that those scientists who wish to make patent claims must be able to move freely between two distinct worlds, each with its own set of standards, concepts, and rules. There is also the disturbing feeling for those who are accustomed to being judged by their scientific peers that, in the patenting worlds, their judges will be lawyers who will define the criteria by which a claim is judged. Also, a research summary for a patent claim has to be written in legal terminology for an entirely different kind of audience. Occasionally, new experiments may have to be performed to obtain conformatory evidence or to settle disputes and counterclaims by competitors. In the British survey, scientists were found to use patents for a number of purposes: to maintain and further their credibility among their peers, to initiate and maintain their connections with firms and other entities

---

[2]Examples are the discovery of a new species, or of an important natural phenomenon such as the discovery of gravity by Newton, or the theory of relativity by Einstein. In this sense, many important discoveries in a number of basic sciences, such as astronomy, are not patentable.

outside the university, to further their position within the university faculty, and to obtain additional support for their research programs, and so on.

An important element in filling patent claims is the correct sense of timing to ensure that it will attract sufficient industrial attention without preempting possible future claims when further data become available. This is true of scientific publications as well except for the fact that an earlier publication in a scientific journal does not preempt later publications on the same subject. If a scientist's patent claim is reflected by a patent examiner or a court, it does not reflect on the quality of the research that was presented to support that claim. However, it is well known that, quite often, the implications of the rejection of a scientific paper by a journal are quite different with respect to the quality of that paper, although personal disputes and scientific differences play some part as well. In summary, there appears to be a cyclical process by which the novelty of science is being transformed into a novelty of patenting, which, in turn, leads to additional scientific novelty (Packer and Webster, 1996).

4 Patenting of micro-organisms: the Chakrabarty case

Patenting micro-organisms and cells is not a recent phenomenon. Louis Pasteur was awarded a patent in 1873 (U.S. Patent number 141,072). One of its claims was a yeast, as an article of manufacture free from disease. This was the first of many "living matter" patents that were issued in the United States. The U.S. Congress specifically enacted the Plant Patent Act of 1930 which permitted patent protection for asexually reproduced plants (35 U.S.C. 101).

"Man-made" organisms

The first patent for a "man-made" micro-organism was approved in 1980, by the U.S. Supreme Court in a 5-4 decision in the case of Chakrabarty v. Diamond for a bacterium (*Pseudomonas aeruginosa*) engineered to break down four of the main components of crude oil. This marked a new beginning for patenting "man-made" living organisms. It was based on the premise that the patent legislation, which was earlier enacted by the U.S. Congress, did not distinguish between "living" and "non-living" matter. Until then, micro-organisms were considered to be products of nature and thus not patentable.

In view of the uniqueness of the Chakrabarty patent, this subject is discussed in some detail below.

Ananda Chakrabarty was a microbiologist at the General Electric Research and Development Center in Schenectady, New York. The bacterium, which he had developed to break down multiple compounds of crude oil, was a genetically engineered but not recombinant organism. Because of its unique function in breaking down crude oil, Chakrabarty filed a patent application, which claimed: "These micro-organisms contain at least two stable (compatible) energy generating plasmids, these plasmids specifying degradative pathways".

There were three types of patent claims:
- (a) process claims for the method of producing the bacteria;
- (b) claims for an inoculum comprised of a carrier material floating on water, such as straw, etc.; and
- (c) product claims for the bacteria.

The patent examiner allowed the first two claims but rejected the third on the grounds that micro-organisms are "products of nature", and, as living beings, micro-organisms are not patentable under 35 U.S.C. 101. However, upon appealing to the PTO Board of Appeals, the Board reversed the examiner's decision on the first ground, that the new bacteria were not products of nature because *Pseudomonas* bacteria containing two or more different energy-generating plasmids are not naturally occurring. However, the second ground of rejection, that the bacteria did not constitute statutorily protectable subject matter, was not reversed.

Chakrabarty appealed again, this time to the Court of Customs and Patent Appeals, which reversed the PTO decision. It was then appealed to the Supreme Court, which held, in a 5-4 ruling, that a live, human-made micro-organism is patentable subject matter under section 101 as a "manufacture" or "composition of matter".

The Court's decision is based on the following reasons:

(a) Plain meaning of the statutory language: While emphasizing that words are to be interpreted in their common or contemporary meaning, the Court ruled that courts should not read into the patent laws limitations which the legislature had not specifically expressed. Congress intended that the patent laws should be interpreted in the widest sense possible and such terms as "manufacture" and "composition of matter" must be interpreted according to their ordinary dictionary definitions.

(b) Legislative history of the patent statute: Jefferson's view that "ingenuity should receive a liberal encouragement" was originally adopted by the Congress. the original statutory language remained intact through several rewrites which spanned 187 years.

(c) Recognition of human ingenuity: Natural resources such as new materials discovered in the earth as well as such famous laws as Newton's law of gravity and Einstein's law of $E=mc^2$ were cited as "manifestations of ... nature, free to all men and reversed exclusively to none". On the other hand, Chakrabarty's invention was recognized as a product of human ingenuity.

(d) Plant Patent Act of 1930: This act provided protection for certain asexually reproducing plants. Later on, the Plant Variety Protection Act of 1970 provided protection for certain sexually reproducing plants. However, neither act indicates congressional understanding that the terms "manufacture" or "composition of matter" do not include living organisms.

(e) Genetic terminology: When congress enacted Section 101, genetic terminology was not foreseen as patentable subject matter.

(f) Potential hazards: Arguments against patentability based on potential hazards due to genetic research should be addressed to the Congress and the Executive, not to the Judiciary.

The Chakrabarty patent provided the judicial framework for PTO to determine later that plants and animals were patentable subject matter under the U.S. code. It is generally agreed that the Chakrabarty case provided great economic stimulus to patenting of micro-organisms and cells, and provided a great incentive for the growth of the biotechnology industry.

Commercialization of biotechnology

By assuring the commercialization of biotechnology the Chakrabarty patent stimulated increased research and development. For a fledgling biotechnology company, patents can make all the difference between success and failure. Patents can help attract venture capital, encourage potential collaborators, and create new directions in research and development. Investors react quickly to new patent development. Success of biotechnology during the 1980s can be appreciated from the following facts. By 1987, 403 American companies dedicated to biotechnology and 70 established corporations with significant investments in biotechnology created 35,900 jobs.

Patenting a process

While the Chakrabarty patent dealt with the patentability of an end product, i.e. a human-made micro-organism, several other patents involve the use of such micro-organisms and cells in *processes* that could be patented. In the area of genetic engineering, patents of this kind may refer to processes for producing a stable, inheritable change in the genotype of a living organism. Structural changes in a gene or incorporation of recombinant or reconstituted genetic material can induce such changes. The best known patent of this kind is U.S. Patent number 4,237,224, awarded to Stanley Cohen and Herbert Boyer at Stanford University and University of California at San Francisco, respectively, in 1980. It involved a process for inserting foreign genetic material into a bacterial plasmid, a well known technique in recombinant DNA research.

5 Different types of biotechnological innovations

Biotechnological innovations fall into several classes, depending largely on the technique and the type of tissue involved. Earlier organismic methods gave way in recent years to cellular and molecular methods. Bent et al (1987) considered six types of biotechnological motivations.

Plant varieties

Although it was not until the 19th century that systematic studies of cross-breeding and inbreeding were practiced to improve various food crops, human attempts to manipulate plant material to improve certain desirable characteristics date back to antiquity. The advent of Mendelian genetics and, in recent years, molecular and tissue culture methods have rapidly revolutionized the improvement of commercially important crops. Traditionally plant breeding methods have employed cross-breeding and back-crossing, selection for desirable characteristics followed by inbreeding to stabilize improved lines. Later on, other methods including induction of mutations and polyploidy by using chemical agents or radiation, somatic cell fusion, plant tissue culturing and regeneration have been employed to increase variability.

Genetic engineering and transgenic techniques have radically altered our ability to manipulate the germplasm. Interrelationships among genes are being studied with the aid of recombinant DNA sequences. In virus-related engineering, mutated and chimeral viral genomic sequences are often used in studying viral-gene functions and to convert viral sequences into efficient expression vectors. The study of individual viral genes has led to their introduction and expression in plants. Several recent reviews have dealt with the production of virus-resistant transgenic plants (Sela, 1996).

The greatest challenge facing plant breeders remains the aggregation of desirable traits, such as high yield, disease- and pest-resistance, hardiness, and shorter time to maturity, into a single "variety". The term "variety" refers to a distinct group of plants within the same species that share a number of characteristics which are passed on from one generation to the next and which differentiate the plants of one variety from those of another.

At lease three major factors complicate the process of achieving the desirable goals: (a) multigenic inheritance (as opposed to simpler 'monogenic' inheritance) that is normally associated with such traits as "yield" and "disease-resistance", (b) lack of positive correlation among various desirable traits, and (c) the impact of various environmental factors.

Animal varieties

In contrast to the much-discussed "plant breeder's rights", there do not appear to be any treaty or agreement to secure "animal breeder's rights" anywhere in the world. There are several factors that are common to both plant and animal breeders. The development of "varieties" with several desirable characteristics is similar to both plant and animal species. However, the same obstructions which were mentioned in relation to plant breeding, e.g. multigenic basis, lack of positive correlation among various desirable characters, and the impact of environmental factors, are also true of animal breeding. However, there are some profound differences as well. Asexual reproduction, which is quite common among plants, is a rarity in the animal kingdom. A second feature is the ever present genetic variability which is often expressed under "stressful" conditions. Plant genomes are particularly unstable, readily responding to environmental changes and generating variability in a single generation, whereas the propensity for instability is less characteristic of animals. The latter clearly show a high degree of homeostasis against changes in the environment. Higher animals have a greater control over environments, whereas plants are always at the mercy of the weather. The disruptive effects of sexual reproduction and genetic recombination are often overshadowed by the greater stability of animal genomes, especially under domestication (Bent et al, 1987).

Cell hybrids and cell lines

Fusion of different somatic (non-sexual) cell types are widely practiced for various purposes (e.g. monoclonal antibodies). An important step in the development of this method is the recognition and characterization of the desired end product from a great number of variants generated by cell fusion. However, powerful selection techniques are available for the elimination of undesired somatic cell fusion products. Cell hybrids can be selected for one or two specific cellular characteristics such as antibiotic resistance. In only a few steps, the background variability can be eliminated by selecting for the desired hybrids, a process that would normally take several generations in plant or animal breeding.

Macromolecules and viral particles

This group includes (a) deoxyribonucleic acid (DNA) and ribonucleic acid (RNA) polymers that encode information (hence, *informational* macromolecules) and (b) infectious vectors or viral particles, which are mainly composed of nucleic acid polymers and certain specific protein subunits. These two inventions are not capable of self-replication except under specially controllable conditions inside a host cell. Second, they can be assembled *de novo* from precisely defined constituent elements. using this method, Khorana (1979) demonstrated the total synthesis of a gene.

Manipulation of the basic genetic material that determines and defines various valuable characteristics in all living organisms is becoming much more sophisticated. The nature of inventions involving these macromolecules involve a "reprogramming" of the basic machinery of the cell toward the goal of synthesizing a desired protein. With reference to human gene therapy, W. French Anderson and Michael Blaese have recently obtained patents for the successful transfer of DNA segments but their claims are being challenged by others. Several possible vectors have been developed for the insertion of recombinant genetic material into various cells and tissues. In some cases, direct injection of DNA into the host cell's nucleus has been attempted with limited success. Whatever system may be used for transferring the genetic material a successful expression of the encoded information in the cells of the host organism is generally regarded as a biotechnological invention, especially so when it has clinical and commercial applications.

"Engineered" organisms

May new variants of plants and animals, including micro-organisms, are the recipients of systematically manipulated genetic material in one form or another. they may be regarded as "contrived" or "engineered" to achieve a specific goal. Other forms of "biological engineering" may not involve an alteration of the genetic material. An example cited by Bent et al (1987) involves the introduction of a symbiotic micro-organism into the rumen of an Australian steer, thus rendering it to degrade toxic metabolites of certain shrubs.

"Pure" cultures of unmodified, naturally occurring cells

Commercial use of unmodified bacterial and yeast cultures dates back to ancient times. In recent years, animal and plant cells and tissues have been used to synthesize pharmacological compounds. The technique often consists of isolating certain cells from nature and propagating them to establish "pure" cultures. As Bent et al (1987) put it: "the applied biologist who seeks to develop a new pure culture must take his starting material–a mix of cell types sampled from a preexisting local ecology".

All biotechnological inventions go through the same developmental stages–exploring variability, replication, and application of selection criteria. Bent et al (1987) have argued that, for the purpose of industrial property protection, there are no technological reasons for subjecting each type of biotechnological invention to *sui generis* treatment under the laws governing intellectual property rights.

Examples of patent claims in biotechnology

(Summarized from *The Law and Strategy of Biotechnology Patents* by Kenneth D. Sibley, Butterworth-Heinemann, London, 1994.)

I. Materials isolated from nature
 (1) Pasteur's patent on yeast is an early example of a naturally occurring organism–"Yeast, free from organic germs of disease, as an article of manufacture".

(2) A recent example–New England Medical Center patent for *Lactobacillus* species–said bacteria being characterized in that they have the same ability to attach mucosal cells of the human intestinal tract as that exhibited by the *Lactobacillus* bacteria deposited in the American Type Culture Collection (Accession No. 53103).

(3) Example of a patent on a naturally occurring protein isolated from nature is the Genetics Institute's patent for erythropoietin. However, this claim was held invalid as too broad and indefinite when challenged by Amgen. The Amgen claims to isolated DNA encoding erythropoietin that were held valid include the following:
1. A purified and isolated DNA sequence consisting essentially of a DNA sequence encoding human erythropoietin . . . and
2. A procaryotic or eucaryotic host cell transformed or transfected with a DNA sequence . . . in a manner allowing the host cell to express erythropoietin.

(4) Systemix patent for human hematopoietic stem cells.

II. Biotechnology techniques

(1) Cohen and Boyer patent issued to Stanford University (1980), for Recombinant DNA procedures, (the patent had been pending since 1974):
1. A method for replicating a biologically functional DNA, which comprises:
    transforming under transforming conditions compatible unicellular organisms with biologically functional DNA prepared in vitro by the method of:
    (a) cleaving a viral or circular plasmid DNA compatible with said unicellular organisms to provide a first linear segment having an intact replicon and termini of a predetermined character;
    (b) combining said first linear segment with a second linear DNA segment, having at least one intact gene and foreign to said unicellular organism and having termini ligatable to said termini of said first linear segment, wherein at least one of said first and second linear DNA segments has a gene for a phenotypical trait, under joining conditions where the termini of said first and second segments join to provide a functional DNA capable of replication and transcription in said unicellular organism;
    (c) growing said unicellular organisms under appropriate nutrient conditions; and isolating said transformants from said parent unicellular

organisms by means of said phenotypical trait imparted by said biologically functional DNA.

2. A method according to claim 1, wherein said unicellular organisms are bacteria.

3. A counterpart to Cohen and Boyer's patent was issued in 1988, to include additional methods and products.

(2) A patent for cloning vehicle was issued to Genentech in 1987. It had been pending in various forms for ten years:

1. A recombinant DNA cloning vehicle suited for transformation of a microbial host comprising:

(a) a homologous control region which regulates expression of a structural gene and

(b) a DNA insert comprising codons for a preselected functional heterologous polypeptide or polypeptide intermediate therefore characterized in that the DNA insert is operably linked to and in proper reading frame relative to the said control region and the host transformed thereby is capable of expressing the preselected heterologous polypeptide or polypeptide intermediate therefore under the control of the said control region and in recoverable form.

2. A recombinant cloning vehicle according to claim 1 wherein the control region is essentially identical to a control region ordinarily present in the chromosomal DNA of a bacterial species that serves as the host for transformation.

3. A recombinant cloning vehicle according to claim 2 wherein said polypeptide is the A chain of human insulin.

(3) Cornell University's "gene gun" patent:

A method for introducing particles into cells comprising accelerating particles having a diameter sufficiently small to penetrate and be retained in a preselected cell without killing the cell, and propelling said particles at said cells whereby said particles penetrate the surface of said cells and become incorporated into the interior of said cells.

(4) A Kary Mullis polymerase chain reaction (PCR) patent:

1. A process for amplifying at least one specific nucleic acid sequence contained in a nucleic acid consists of two separate complementary strands, of equal or unequal length, which process comprises:

(a) treating the strands with two oligonucleotide primers, for each different specific sequence being amplified, under conditions such that for each different sequence being amplified an extension product of each primer is synthesized which is complimentary to each nucleic acid strand, wherein said primers are selected so as to be sufficiently complimentary to different strands of each specific sequence to hybridize therewith such that the extension product synthesized from one primer, when it is separated from its complement, can serve as a template for synthesis of the extension product of the other primer;
(b) separating the primer extension products from the templates on which they were synthesized to produce single-stranded molecules; and
(c) treating the single-stranded molecules generated from step (a) under conditions that a primer extension product is synthesized using each of the single strands produced in step (b) as a template.

III. Diagnostic techniques
Two examples are given below.
(1) Falkow and Moseley patent for DNA probes:
A method for detecting the presence of a pathogen in a clinical sample suspected of containing said pathogen, said method comprising:
1. depositing said sample on an inert support;
2. treating said sample to affix genetic material of any of said pathogen present in said sample to said support in substantially single stranded form at substantially the same site on said support where said sample was deposited;
3. contacting said fixed single stranded material with a labeled probe having at least substantially complementary to a nucleotide sequence of a structural gene characteristic of said pathogen, said contacting being under hybridizing conditions at a predetermined stringency; and
4. detecting duplex formation on said support by means of said label.

(2) Hybritech monoclonal sandwich assay patent:
A process for the determination of the presence or concentration of an antigenic substance in a fluid comprising the steps of:
1. contacting a sample of the fluid with a measured amount of a soluble first monoclonal antibody to the antigenic substance in order to form a soluble complex of the antibody and antigenic

substance present in said sample, said first monoclonal antibody being labeled;
2. contacting the soluble complex with a second monoclonal antibody to the antigenic substance, said second monoclonal antibody being bound to a solid carrier, said solid carrier being insoluble in said fluid, in order to form an insoluble complex of said first monoclonal antibody, said antigenic substance and said second monoclonal antibody bound to said solid carrier; etc.

IV. Plant science
Some claims in the first utility patent for plants *per se*:

(1) A monocotyledonous plant capable of producing seed having an endogenous free tryptophan content of at least about one-tenth milligram per gram dry seed weight, wherein the seed is capable of germinating into a plant capable of producing seed having an endogenous free tryptophan content of at least about one-tenth milligram per gram dry seed weight.

(2) Other examples of Patents found on plants *per se* include hybrid corn issued to Pioneer Hi-Bred:

(1) Hybrid corn seed designated 3471.
(2) A hybrid corn plant and its plant parts produced by the seeds of claim 1.
...
(4) A hybrid corn plant with the phenotypic characteristics of the hybrid plant.

(3) A different kind of patent is the one filed by Calgene for the use of the polygalacturonase gene in antisense to control the ripening of plants such as tomato:

(a) A DNA construct comprising of at least 15 base pairs of a DNA sequence encoding tomato polygalacturonase (PG) joined, in the opposite orientation for expression, 5' to the 3' terminus of a transcriptional initiation region functional in plants.
(b) A tomato plant cell comprising a DNA construct according to (a).

V. Animal science
The following are some examples:

(1) An Ohio University patent for the genetic transformation of zygotes.
(2) The "Harvard mouse patent", the first patent on an animal *per se*, reads as follows:

(a) A transgenic non-human mammal all of whose germ cells and somatic cells contain a recombinant activated oncogene sequence introduced into said mammal, or an ancestor of said mammal, at an embryonic stage.
(b) The mammal of claim (a), a chromosome of said mammal including an endogenous coding sequence substantially the same as a coding sequence of said oncogene sequence.
(c) The mammal of claim (a), said mammal being a rodent.
(d) The mammal of claim (a), said rodent being a mouse.

We might also consider the Biogen patent for the production of recombinant proteins in animal milk which includes claims to a manufacturing process utilizing a transgenic mammal.

VI. Therapeutic compounds, methods, and compositions

These patents include compounds, new therapeutic methods of treatment, and compositions for treating several diseases in all living organisms including human populations as well as various plant animal species.

(1) One example is a method to combat retroviruses which involves administering to host a composition comprising an inhibitory effective amount of a peptide of 3 to about 11 amino acids containing the amino acid sequence Phe-X-Gly, wherein X is any amino acid. (Patent issued to Research Corporation.)

(2) Another example is an NYU patent for live vaccines for the treatment of bacterial-mediated diarrheal diseases such as cholera and typhoid:

A plasmid which comprises a gene coding for an immunologically active, conjugably transferable, non-toxic heat-labile *Escherichia coli* enterotoxin and a gene coding for a non-toxic, heat-stable *Escherichia coli* enterotoxin.

6 International treaties

The following is a brief outline of the history of international treaties regarding patents and plant varieties.

The Paris Union Convention

Until June 1, 1978, applicants filing for foreign patents depended upon the rights granted by the Paris Union Convention, especially article 4 of the Convention which provides for the "right of priority". This right enables any resident or national of a member country to file a patent application in any member country and then file a patent application for the same invention in another country under the treaty, the additional patents will be treated as if they were filed on the same date as the first patent application, as long as the later patent applications were filed within twelve months of the first patent application. As of June 1, 1978, applications have been accepted under the European Patent Convention (EPC) and also the Patent Cooperation Treaty (PCT), enabling the applicants to enjoy the benefit of the right of priority.

The PCT is a worldwide convention which is open to membership by any member of the Paris Union. The main objective is to simplify the foreign filing of patent applications and reduce the cost by avoiding a duplication of multiple filings. After completing an international search, each search report and a copy of the application are distributed to the patent office in each member country by the World Intellectual Property Organization (WIPO) in Geneva.

The EPC established a single supra-national European Patent Office (EPO) and a uniform procedural system which exists in addition to the conventional national granting procedures and national patents. The main goal is to streamline the procedures, establish a uniform law of patents for Europe, and develop patent protection in Europe. A second convention, the Community Patent Convention (CPC), provides for a single patent covering the entire territory of the European Community (EC).

The Paris Convention was signed on March 20, 1883, and entered into force on July 7, 1884. It has been revised at least nine times since then. The Paris Union is a universal (worldwide) treaty, establishing certain basic rights for protection of property. It is concerned with a wide variety of industrial patents. The right of priority and the 12-month priority period are particularly relevant to biological inventions because it enables an applicant to satisfy the tissue culture deposit requirements that are required by certain countries which do not recognize the deposits made in foreign countries.

The Budapest Treaty

The Budapest Treaty became effective on August 19, 1980. The complete title of the Budapest Treaty is "Budapest Treaty on the International Recognition of the Deposit of Micro-organisms for the Purposes of Patent Procedure". It is open to membership for any country that belongs to the Paris Union Convention. Its major aim is to provide recognition, for the purpose of their own patents, by the member states of a deposit of the micro-organism strain which is made in another country of the Treaty. Its provisions include a series of International Depository Authorities (IDA) which are depository institutions located in a member country and are recognized by the appropriate national or international organizations (WIPO) that the institution guarantees compliance with a number of regulations as required by the Treaty. However, the Treaty did not specify the details of the micro-organism deposits. These are left to the discretion of the domestic laws of the relevant country.

The following information is required with the original deposit:

(1) the name and address of the IDA,
(2) the name and address of the depositor,
(3) the date of the original deposit,
(4) the identification reference,
(5) the accession number of the deposit, and
(6) the scientific description of the deposit.

The Treaty further allows the depositor to make a "new deposit" of the same micro-organism if the original deposit is no longer viable (e.g. when it exceeds the five-year minimum limit) or when limited by some other restrictions such as those dealing with imports and exports, etc. Other provisions cover viability tests, secrecy, availability of samples to third parties, and recognition by all member countries, etc.

If certain deposits were made before the depository institution acquired the status of an IDA, they may be converted to deposit under the treaty upon receiving a written request from the depositor who must then provide all the required information to qualify for deposit and acceptance.

The basic disclosure requirement under the European Patent Convention (EPC) reads as follows: "The European patent application must disclose the invention in a manner sufficiently clear and complete for it to be carried out by a person skilled in the art". The description should contain a statement of invention in terms of technical problem and its solution, a detailed description, using example drawings where appropriate, and its capability of exploitation in industry. Certain other aspects, such as statements that may disparage other products or individuals, are clearly prohibited.

Convention on Biological Diversity

The Convention on Biological Diversity (CBD) was negotiated before the United Nations Conference on Environment and Development (UNCED) held in Rio de Janeiro in 1992. It became effective on 29 December 1993. Plans for the Convention on Biological Diversity (CBD) began in 1987 when the Governing council of UNEP established an Ad Hoc Working Group of Experts on Biological Diversity which met in 1988. The agreed text of the CBD was adopted by 101 governments in Nairobi in May 1992 and signed by 159 governments and the European Union at the United Nations Conference on Environment and Development (UNCED) which was held in Rio de Janeiro in June 1992. The first meeting of the conference was held in Bahamas in 1994.

The objectives of the Convention are stated, in part, as follows in its Article 1:

> conservation of biological diversity, the sustainable use of its components and the fair and equitable sharing of benefits arising out of the utilization of genetic resources, including by appropriate access to genetic resources and by appropriate transfer of relevant technologies

Article 2 defines "Biological Diversity" as follows:

> "Biological Diversity" means the variability among living organisms from all sources, including, inter alia, terrestrial, marine and other aquatic ecosystems and

the ecological complexes of which they are part; this includes diversity within species, between species and of ecosystems.

Consequently, there are several different levels of biodiversity which may be due to different mechanisms such as mutational, chromosomal, adaptational, and geographic–all leading to the creation of new species, subspecies, varieties, and so on. Similarly, gene dispersal and hybridization in nature also contribute to biological diversity. The disciplines involved in studying biodiversity are evolutionary biology, taxonomy, ecology, genetics, population biology, and biochemistry to forces which contribute to the creation of reproductive barriers, eventually leading to the appearance of new varieties and species.

Biodiversity is an index of the biological wealth of this planet. Many species have become extinct, especially in the last few centuries when industrialization began on a large scale. Although new species and varieties are occasionally created, the rate of loss of biodiversity is far greater than the gain. Table 6.4 gives the number of recorded species which have become extinct since 1600.

The Global Biodiversity convention became effective on December 29, 1993. In part, it states:

> States have sovereign rights over their own biological resources, . . . States are responsible for conserving their biological diversity and for using their biological resources in a sustainable manner.

Prof. Swaminathan (1995) has drawn attention to certain exclusions from the agreed version of the GATT (Uruguay round). For instance, under section 3 of Article 27, we find:

> Members may also exclude from patentability:
> (a) diagnostic, therapeutic and surgical methods for the treatment of humans or animals;
> (b) plants and animals other than micr-oorganisms, and essentially biological processes for the production of plants or animals other than non-biological and microbiological processes. However, Members shall provide for the protection of plant varieties either by patents or by an effective *sui generis* system or by any combination thereof.

Protection of new varieties of plants (UPOV)

Plant Breeders' Rights (PBR) have been recognized and practiced in the industrialized countries for many years. The importance of protecting biological inventions was recognized at least as early as the Paris Convention of 1883. The concept of protecting "industrial property" was also meant to include agricultural products such as wines, grain, fruit, cattle, etc.

The Act of London of June 2, 1934, of the Paris Convention expanded the scope of "industrial property".Article I (3) specified that:

> Industrial property shall be understood in the broadest sense and likewise to agricultural and extractive industries and to all manufactured or natural products; for example, wines, grains, tobacco leaf, fruit, cattle, minerals, mineral waters, beer, flowers, and flour.

However, there was widespread skepticism about any attempts to protect plant varieties, partly due to fears that it may lead to controlled food shortages and increase food costs because of monopolies which a patentee would enjoy. However, a number of European countries passed separate legislation in the nature of variety protection rights, which were quite distinct from the exclusive rights granted by the patent laws. But the nature and extent of these variety protection rights varied greatly from country to country in Europe. In France, in addition to protecting a new plant variety to a limited extent, it was also possible to obtain a utility patent for a breeding process. In several countries including Germany, Spain and Italy, the patent laws before 1950 granted protection for breeding methods, and, in a few cases, the resulting plant variety also. In Italy, high Court decisions in 1948 and 1950 granted patent protection for new plant varieties, within the context of "industrial results".

In Germany, "seed protection" laws were enacted as early as 1883. The seed registration system eventually became a model in the 1930s for a national system administered by the German federal government. A draft version of a "Seed and Plant Stock Law" was promulgated by the Ministry of Food and Agriculture on January 15, 1930, but it was dropped when the National Socialists came to power in 1933. After World War II, serious efforts were initiated in West Germany to recognize plant varieties as legitimately patentable subject matter.

The International Association for the Protection of Industrial Property ('Association Internationale pour la Protection de la Propriete Industrielle' or

AIPPI), at its London Congress in 1932, had already discussed the need for protection of new plant varieties. By the time of the Vienna Congress in 1952, Germany was ready to present a comprehensive report on the issue of protecting plant-related inventions, with proposals for changes to Articles 1 and 4 of the London text of the Paris Convention on Intellectual Property. The German delegation submitted the following resolution to the Vienna Congress:

> (1) A legal protection should be provided for plants having new properties which are important for their exploitation, provided that reproducibility of these plants is ensured.
> (2) The application of an invention in agriculture, forestry, horticulture and similar fields should be made equivalent to the industrial application of an invention as required in the Patent Laws of many countries.

From a historical perspective, the German proposal was important because it recognized the fact that biological inventions arising from agriculture were not adequately protected by the patent laws of many countries. It recognized further that inventions in the field of plant breeding that met the criteria of industrial applicability warrant protection under the Patent Law.

However, the Vienna Congress did not allot sufficient time to discuss the German proposals in detail, and the question was tabled again. The International Association of Plant Breeders for the Protection of Plant Varieties ('Association Internationale des Selectionneurs pour la Protection des Obtentions Vegetales,' or ASSINSEL) at its Vienna-Semmering Conference in 1956 accepted a proposal from the French delegate that France should hold an International Conference for the Protection of New Plant Products. Consequently, the First International Conference for the Protection of new Plant Products was held in Paris in May, 1957. Participating countries included Federal Republic of Germany, Austria, Belgium, Denmark, Spain, Finland, Italy, Norway, The Netherlands, the United Kingdom, Sweden and Switzerland. The Conference reconciled 'varietal protection' with 'seed registration' and emphasized the need to create a new "union" apart from the Paris Convention. The conference delegated the task of working out further details to a Committee of Experts, which eventually led to the UPOV Convention of Paris in 1961.

International Union for the Protection of New Varieties of Plants (UPOV, Paris, 1961)

The UPOV Convention of Paris was initially signed on December 2, 1961, by Belgium, Denmark, France, the Federal Republic of Germany, The Netherlands, Italy, and the United Kingdom. The Convention became effective when three countries, the Federal Republic of Germany, The Netherlands, and the United Kingdom, ratified the Convention on August 10, 1968.

The most significant stipulations of UPOV (1961) were as follows:

(1) The new variety must be clearly distinct from any other commonly known variety,
(2) The new variety must be homogeneous and stable,
(3) The new variety was not previously offered for sale,
(4) The new variety can be protected either by a patent or by a special title of protection,
(5) The new variety must be given a suitable varietal denomination,
(6) The term of protection may not be less than 15 years, and for some species (such as fruit trees, vines, forest tress and ornamental trees) the minimum period of protection is 18 years.

The Convention was revised at least three times up to 1991. It was useful in providing protected varieties to plant breeders and farmers. However, to meet breeders' and farmers' changing needs, UPOV Convention had undergone a significant change in 1991; it eliminated the breeder's exemption from a variety (called "essentially derived variety"), that is predominantly derived from another variety but retains the essential genetic content of the original variety.

By 1993, UPOV had 22 members: Australia, Belgium, Canada, Czech Republic, Denmark, France, Germany, Hungary, Ireland, Israel, Italy, Japan, Netherlands, New Zealand, Poland, Slovak Republic, South Africa, Spain, Sweden, Switzerland, United Kingdom and the U.S.A. Several other countries have started procedures which will eventually enable them to become effective members. The advent of molecular biology has made it even more imperative that all countries should join UPOV immediately.

Table 6.1 Comparison of PBR under the UPOV Convention and Patent Law

Provisions	UPOV 1978 Act	UPOV 1991 Act	Patent Law
Protection Coverage	Plant varieties of nationally defined species	Plant varieties of all genera and species	Inventions
Requirements	Distinctness Uniformity Stability	Novelty Distinctness Uniformity Stability	Novelty Inventiveness Non-obviousness Industrial application, usefulness
Protection term	Min. 15 Yrs	Min. 20 Yrs	17-20 Yrs (OECD)
Protection scope	Commercial use of reproductive material of the variety	Commercial use of all material of the variety	Commercial use of protected matter
Breeders' exemption	Yes	Not for essentially derived varieties	No
Farmers' privilege	In practice: yes	Up to National laws	No
Prohibition of double protection	Any species eligible for PBR protection cannot be patented	–	–

Source: M.S. Swaminathan, 1995

Table 6.2 Number of threatened species

Species	Endangered	Vulnerable	Total
Mammals	177	199	376
Birds	188	241	429
Reptiles	47	88	135
Amphibians	32	32	64
Fishes	158	226	384
Invertebrates	582	702	1284
Plants	3632	5687	9319
Total	**4816**	**7175**	**11991**

Source: The World Conservation Monitoring Center, 1995

Table 6.3 Systems of biodiversity

Group	Nature of Diversity	Mechanism
Species	Evolutionary	Mutational
Subspecies	Ecological	Chromosomal
Populations	Genetic	Hybridization
Individuals	Biochemical Molecular	Selection and Geographic adaptation

Table 6.4 Number of recorded species that have been extinct since 1600

Group	Number extinct	
Molluscs	191	
Birds	115	
Mammals	58	
Other animals	120	
Total animals		484
Plants		654
Grand total		1138

Source: Heywood, 1995

Table 6.5 International agreements

Treaty	Entered into Force	Number of Signatories
Budapest Treaty	Aug. 19, 1980	22
Patent Cooperation Treaty	Jan. 24, 1978	40
European Patent Convention	Oct. 7, 1977	13
Union for the Protection of New Varieties of Plants	Aug. 10, 1968	17
Paris Union Convention	July 7, 1884	97

Source: Office of Technology Assessment, 1989

Table 6.6 Member countries, Budapest Treaty on the International Recognition of Micro-organisms for the Purposes of Patent Procedure

Australia	Republic of Korea
Austria	Liechtenstein
Belgium	Netherlands
Bulgaria	Norway
Denmark	Philippines
Finland	Soviet Union
France	Spain
Federal Republic of Germany	Sweden
Hungary	Switzerland
Italy	United Kingdom
Japan	United States

Source: Office of Technology Assessment, 1989

Table 6.7 Member countries, European Patent Convention

Austria	Liechtenstein
Belgium	Luxembourg
France	Netherlands
Federal Republic of Germany	Spain
Great Britain	Sweden
Greece	Switzerland
Italy	

Source: Office of Technology Assessment, 1989

Table 6.8 Member countries, Paris Union Convention

Algeria	Holy See
Argentina	Hungary
Australia	Iceland
Austria	Indonesia
Bahamas	Iran
Barbados	Iraq
Belgium	Ireland
Benin	Israel
Brazil	Italy
Bulgaria	Ivory Coast
Burkina Faso	Japan
Burundi	Jordan
Cameroon	Kenya
Canada	Democratic People's Rep. of Korea
Central African Republic	Republic of Korea
Chad	Lebanon
China	Libya
Congo	Liechtenstein
Cuba	Luxembourg
Cyprus	Madagascar
Czechoslovakia	Malawi
Denmark	Malta
Dominican Republic	Mauritania
Egypt	Mauritius
Finland	Mexico
France	Monaco
Gabon	Mongolia
German Democratic Republic	Morocco
Federal Republic of Germany	Netherlands
Ghana	New Zealand
Greece	Niger
Guinea	Nigeria
Guinea-Bissau	Norway
Haiti	Philippines

Table 6.8 Member countries, Paris Union Convention (continued)

Poland
Portugal
Romania
Rwanda
San Marino
Senegal
South Africa
Soviet Union
Spain
Sri Lanka
Sudan
Suriname
Sweden
Switzerland
Syria
United Republic of Tanzania
Togo
Trinidad and Tobago
Tunisia
Turkey
Uganda
United Kingdom
United States
Uruguay
Viet Nam
Yugoslavia
Zaire
Zambia
Zimbabwe

Source: Office of Technology Assessment, 1989

Table 6.9 Member countries, Patent Cooperation Treaty (PCT)

Australia	Republic of Korea
Austria	Liechtenstein
Belgium	Luxembourg
Benin	Madagascar
Brazil	Malawi
Bulgaria	Mali
Cameroon	Mauritania
Central African Republic	Monaco
Chad	Netherlands
Congo	Norway
Denmark	Romania
Finland	Senegal
France	Soviet Union
Gabon	Sri Lanka
Germany	Sudan
Great Britain	Sweden
Hungary	Switzerland
Italy	Togo
Japan	United States
Democratic People's Rep. of Korea	

Source: Office of Technology Assessment, 1989

Table 6.10 Member countries, Union for the Protection of New Varieties of Plants

Belgium	Netherlands
Denmark	New Zealand
France	South Africa
Federal Republic of Germany	Spain
Hungary	Sweden
Ireland	Switzerland
Israel	United Kingdom
Italy	United States
Japan	

Source: Office of Technology Assessment, 1989

7 Safety considerations for transgenic organisms

In a survey of scientists and institutional regulatory officials who were experienced in fields trials, Hobal and Kendall (1992) found the following facts:

1. Federal regulation of biotechnology in general, and field tests in particular, are necessary given current levels of public concern about safety of biotechnology research.
2. Biosafety protocols currently required for field tests are overly cautious. However, they are necessary to reassure the public.
3. Permitting agencies have shown flexibility in adjusting safety requirements commensurate with the field testing experience of various organisms.
4. Those who are involved with field tests are acutely sensitive to public concerns and go to considerable lengths to provide information about the test to the press, to officials at all levels, and to the public at large.
5. There is an increase in the regulation of biotechnology at the state level, often leading to costly duplication of effort and delays.

In most cases, the pretesting expectations are more than adequately satisfied by the test results.

The following are some concerns that are normally associated with the environmental release of transgenic organisms and plants:

(a) Does the organism have any detrimental effects on plants, animals, or humans?

(b) Does the organism persist in the environment?

(c) Can the organism spread beyond the test plot? (Such as wind dispersal, water dispersal, mechanical dispersal [by animals and humans, etc.], and biological vector dispersal.)

(d) Is the introduced material able to be transferred (gene transfer) to other organisms?

(1) If so, what is the probability of horizontal transfer of the genetic material?

(2) If the gene is transferred, will the new genetic information be maintained and expressed?
(3) What is the known function of the new genetic material?
(4) If the modified micro-organism moves beyond the point of introduction, how will it affect, as a result of the transformation, the surrounding populations or communities of plants, animals, and indigenous microbes?

Gene transfer refers to the spread of genetic material through natural genetic mechanisms. It should be added, however, that little is known about the frequency of genetic exchange in nature. Although this is expected to be rare in nature, Haldane (1958) had considered it to be more frequent when different varieties of crops are planted in mixed plots.

Patenting engineered plants: potential risks to the environment

The fundamental question about safety is, "How does one identify the product, determine its environmental fate, and assess its ecological effects?" Previous experience indicates certain conclusions:

(a) risk is largely defined by the following factors:
  (1) the source of the introduced gene,
  (2) the stability of the introduced gene,
  (3) the activity of gene product, and
  (4) the fate of the engineered gene product in the host plant.

(b) risk evaluation for non-target effects on ecology, health and food safety, varies greatly in each case which should be evaluated separately.

Genetic contamination

As a first step, the isolation, characterization, and tracking of introduced genes as well as the vectors and the gene products facilitates an understanding of the stability and ecological consequences of the introduced gene. The biology of the plant itself plays a significant role in determining the ecological and other effects of the introduced gene. These factors include the means of propagation of the plant, the type of pollen and seed dispersal (and also the duration of viability of the pollen and seed), and if related species exist in the proximity with which the engineered plant can cross-pollinate successfully and produce viable seed. Biological or genetic contamination of the neighboring cultivated plants as well as species is a continuing concern. This subject has been recently reviewed by Watrud et al (1996).

Some preliminary data have indicated that outcrossing may occur to a limited extent in such plants as canola, potato, and cotton, but in some others such as alfalfa and oats it may be much more extensive (Dale et al, 1992; Umbeck et al, 1987; Bing et al, 1991, etc.). Another concern is the possible transfer of the engineered plant DNA to insects, birds and mammals which normally consume some parts of the plant and its possible impact on those animal species. With respect to the fate of engineered gene products in plants, Watrud et al (1996) have commented that little work has been published so far. There is some evidence which indicates that delta-endotoxin when engineered in cotton leaf degrades rapidly (Palm et al, 1994).

Much depends also on the viability and fecundity of the insects which may be infected by the engineered DNA or the vector plant viruses. For virus-resistant plants, the tendency of certain types of viruses to recombine more frequently may impact on the risk involved in predicting the ecological consequences.

Virus-related genetic engineering in plants

Recombinant DNA sequences are used in plants for several purposes: to introduce desirable qualities such as crop yield, disease resistance, herbicide tolerance, and insect resistance, etc., and to study the interrelationships between genes or to study the function of certain sequences in cells.

Sela (1996) reviewed studies of the impact of virus-related engineering on plants. In virus-related engineering, viral genomic sequences are used for the purpose of studying viral-gene functions and for converting viral sequences into efficient expression vectors. Studies of plant transformations by viral and non-viral sequences have been used for generating engineered virus-resistance plants. Virus resistance in plants may be produced when they are transformed with sequences related to the following:

(a) the viral capsid protein,
(b) the viral movement protein,
(c) viral genes for replicases (and putative replicases),
(d) viral genes for proteases,
(e) satellites of viruses and defective interfering RNAs,
(f) anti-sense viral sequences,
(g) ribozymes constructed with viral sequences,
(h) foreign non-viral, non-host genes,
(i) host genes.

Table 7.1 Field tests of genetically engineered crops in the U.S.A.

Traits	Crops
Herbicide tolerance	Soybean
Insect resistance	Potato
Virus resistance	Cotton
Bacterial resistance	Tomato
Fruit development/ ripening	Corn
Altered storage protein	Tobacco
Increased solids	Cantaloupe
Fungal resistance	Squash
Seed oil modifications	Alfalfa
Bruising resistance	Rapeseed
Male sterility	Rice
Altered sweetening	Cucumber
Metal chelation	Chrysanthemum
	Melon
	Walnut
	Papaya
	Poplar
	Serviceberry
	Apple

Source: Modified after Watrud et al, 1996

Stability

A single amino acid substitution in the viral coat protein is sufficient to alter resistance in many cases of natural or engineered resistance. This was reported for tobacco mosaic virus by Knorr and Dawson (1988), for potato virus X by Kohm et al (1993), and for the engineered resistance of alfalfa mosaic virus (Tumer et al, 1991) as well as of cucumber mosaic virus (Nakajima et al, 1993). These findings should be taken into consideration when testing the genetic stability of the resistant phenotypes, especially under field conditions (Sela, 1996).

Risk in releasing virus-related transgenic plants

It has been suggested that new viral strains could potentially arise from releasing artificially protected transgenic plants into the environment and exposing them to inoculation with viruses (De Zoeten, 1991). One method is viral RNA recombination which has been implicated in RNA virus evolution. RNA recombination has been reported for plant viruses. A recombination between a viral RNA and transcripts of a transgenic plant has been reported recently. RNA recombination creates new genotypes which may persist and passes on through several generations, but so far no deleterious effects have been reported. This subject has been reviewed by Sela (1996). Public perception of the benefits and risks involved in the applications of genetic engineering is identified as one of the key determinant of the acceptance and development of biotechnology. Surely such perceptions play a vital role in understanding the issues related to intellectual property rights. In recent years, public awareness of biotechnology has significantly increased through its extensive coverage in the popular media.

Consumer attitudes toward the new technologies have been the subject of opinion poll research by Zechendorf (1994). Nature of the application was found to be a key determinant in shaping public attitudes. Medical applications were found to be more acceptable than food-related applications. This preference was particularly noted in Japan. Furthermore, applications involving animal species were found to be less preferable than those involving plants or micro-organisms. The role of application specificity in shaping public acceptance has been emphasized by several investigators (Frewer et al, 1997; Sparks et al, 1994; Hoban and Kendall, 1992;

Marlier, 1992). Ethical concerns appear to depend on specific applications rather than technology itself (Sparks and Shepherd, 1996). A case-by-case evaluation appears to be the basis for any acceptance by the public (Frewer et al, 1997).

Abstract vs. specific risk

Risk perceptions depend on many factors, among them the nature of the risk itself is the most important. Dramatic or sensation risk tends to be greatly overestimated.

Table 7.2 Number and percentage of approvals* of field trials of engineered plants by traits and by country

Trait	Number of Approvals	% Approved
Herbicide tolerance	483	57
Virus resistance	113	13
Insect resistance	87	10
Quality traits	68	8
Male sterility	39	5
Disease resistance	35	4
Country		
United States	316	37
Canada	302	36
France	77	9
Belgium	62	7
United Kingdom	45	5
Netherlands	22	3
Spain	6	1
Sweden	6	1
Denmark	3	1
Germany	2	1
Switzerland	2	1
Australia	1	1
Japan	1	1
Norway	1	1

*An approval may be for a test in a single site or multiple sites for one year or several years. Some trials include crops with more than one genetically engineered trait.
Source: Levin and Israeli, 1996

Table 7.3 Some examples of gene flow from crops to wild relatives resulting in new or worse weeds

Crop	Wild relative	Result of gene flow
Pearl millet	Wild millet	Shibra, a weed
Sorghum	Johnsongrass	Aggressive johnsongrass
Corn	Teosinte	Weedy types of teosinte
Rice	Wild rice	Weedy rice
Foxtail millet	Wild green foxtail	Weedy giant green foxtail

Source: Levin and Israeli, 1996

Interest in IPR issues itself may be directly related to the perception of the degree of risk itself. It is well known that disparity exists between lay and expert perceptions of risk for a number of situations. This disparity depends on several factors, not the least of which are the public perception of power and the credibility of the risk regulators. Risk perceptions must be viewed within their social context. When exposure to a risk is regarded as involuntary, that risk is then perceived as more threatening than when there is a choice over personal exposure (Sharlin, 1989). Genetically engineered foods may belong to this category because of the inability to distinguish them from the naturally occurring foods.

Freyer et al's (1997) in-depth analysis of risk perceptions with respect to genetic engineering "indicate that different applications of genetic engineering are closely linked to perceptions of risk and benefit or need that are defined by the nature of each application". Most negative reactions have been found in association with genetic engineering, but not the products of these processes. An additional concern centered around a feeling of "unnaturalness" which is associated with applications involving animal and human DNA.

There have been a number of studies which attempted to evaluate the social impact of genetic engineering. In a recent study of public concerns in Great Britain, Frewer et al (1997) listed the following applications of genetic engineering:

General applications:
Genetic engineering of microorganisms for food production
Genetic engineering of plants for food production
Genetic engineering of animals for food production
Transfer of human DNA to other organisms for food production

Genetic engineering of microorganisms for agriculture
Genetic engineering of plants for agriculture
Genetic engineering of animals for agriculture
Transfer of human DNA to other organisms for agriculture
Genetic engineering of microorganisms for medicine
Genetic engineering of plants for medicine
Genetic engineering of animals for medicine
Transfer of human DNA to other organisms for medicine
Genetic engineering of humans for medicine
Genetic "screening" of humans for medicine
Genetic "screening" of humans for non-medicinal purposes

<u>Specific applications:</u>
Herbicide-resistant crops
Test-tube production of human growth hormone
Tomatoes genetically engineered for longevity
Pest-resistant crops
Animals that are modified to facilitate organ transplantation to humans
Beer brewed for cancer research
Strawberries that can grow in frosty conditions
Mice that are specially modified for cancer research
"Vegetarian" cheese
Crops with higher yields
"Screening" for genetic diseases
Salmon that are resistant to lice
Crops modified to grow in arid conditions
Pharmaceutical development and production
Low-fat meat produced by transferring human genes to animals

The question of "need" was also rated as a key ingredient for accepting genetic engineering applications. Perceptions involving the question whether the technology is necessary appear to be more important than perceived risk or ethical concerns. Medical applications tend to be more readily acceptable in terms of importance and need, their final acceptance depending on the perception of an acceptable risk/benefit ratio. Medical applications that did not involve a modification of animal or human genetic material were also seen as the most necessary applications.

In agriculture, perceived need was associated with the production or process rather than specific product characteristics. Genetic modification of certain products was more acceptable because they were considered to be necessary as compared to others. Perceptions of long-term effects were not found to be associated with either acceptance or rejection. Ethical concerns appear to be far more involved with genetic engineering than any other form of technology.

Control is an important characteristic of risk perception. Genetic engineering is perceived as a terminology over which the individual has very little personal control (Frewer et al, 1994). Public acceptance of genetic engineering might depend on both individual risk assessment as well as group assessments. It is not clear to what extent opportunities exist for individuals to contribute to the decision-making process in accepting the new technologies of genetic engineering. The importance of group decision making appears to be widely recognized. The public seems to be able to differentiate between abstract science and science directed at specific events or problems (Michael, 1992).

Transgenic dairy bull

In *Biopolitics*, Vandana Shiva discussed the inconsistent nature of the claims that were associated with the creation of the world's first transgenic dairy bull, Herman, by Gen Pharm, a biotechnology company. Herman was specially bio-engineered by a company scientist to carry a human gene for producing milk with a human protein. When the milk was used in producing an infant formula the safety of that formula was emphasized by stating that the proteins in the milk were made exactly in the same way as in nature. However, when patent claims are made, the same bio-engineered gene and the animal are treated as nonobvious and non-natural, i.e. an artificial product that was created by human ingenuity. According to Shiva, the company claimed that: "Human milk is the gold standard, and formula companies have added more and more (human elements) over the past 20 years" (from *The New Scientist*, 9 January, 1993).

What was even more disturbing, according to Shiva was the changed goal, or perhaps more precisely the broadened goal of the engineered gene that was proposed by the company, Gen Pharm, the creator and owner of Herman. The company's plan to use a modified version of the human transgene in treating cancer and AIDS was approved by an Ethics Board.

Whether a transgene that has been patented with a specific goal can then be modified to suit other applications, especially when it involves such sensitive matters as the production of an infant formula as well as a cure for AIDS is a subject that requires a careful evaluation.

Tracy

Another instance of a commercially exploited transgene was used by Pharmaceutical Proteins Ltd (PPL) to produce the protein alpha-1-antitrypsin in the mammary glands of a sheep, "Tracy". It was described as a "mammalian cell bioreactor". Vandana Shiva commented that the future generations of the animal are clearly not the patent holder's 'inventions'. She wrote: "In claiming the patent, it is the scientist who becomes God, the creator of the patented organism.... (the future generations of the animal) are the product of the organism's regenerative capacity". This criticism is of interest, because if valid, it is applicable to any similar invention. For instance, in human gene therapy, cells engineered with recombinant DNA for the purpose of treating cancer multiply and spread through the tissues. What is patented is the recombinant sequence, not the cell. Consequently, any cell containing that particular sequence is covered by the patent.

Such criticisms seem to be based on a misunderstanding of the biological process. They tend to generate much emotion but clearly do not contribute to a meaningful application of genetics to human welfare. When an evaluation of genetic engineering and patenting is cast against a background of feminism and ecoconcerns, then it is not surprising that the biological issues tend to be overshadowed by other concerns.

Human biology has long been complicated by a miscellaneous collection of social and political concerns. Transgene technology has introduced another complication–economic exploitation–and along with it, risk taking at higher levels. Take, for instance, the genetically engineered maize that was recently developed by Ciba, a Swiss chemicals and pharmaceuticals firm. A gene from the soil bacterium, *Bacillus thuringiensis*, has been transferred to maize (or corn) which makes it resistant to the European corn borer, an insect pest which causes massive damage to the corn each year. The new maize strain has already been approved for cultivation in the U.S., Canada, Japan and some other countries, but the regulators of the European Union (EU) have so far blocked its use. This was mainly due to the complaint of the environmental lobby groups in Europe who labeled it (for some unknown reason) a "mutant"! However, American maize exports to Europe will include small quantities of the genetically engineered maize which is not distinguishable from the usual American maize exports. So this leaves the EU with a peculiar dilemma; either permit the sale of a product which has not been approved by their regulators or ban all American exports altogether.

There is one potential risk that is associated with the maize that has been genetically modified by Ciba. During the course of its development, a marker gene was used to follow its successful genetic transformation, and that marker gene confers resistance to the antibiotics. It is potentially possible that when the cattle or other animals are fed this new strain of maize, the marker gene could infect other bacteria–more dangerous bacteria which could cause fatal diseases in animals as well as humans–which would then become resistant to the antibiotic, but so far this possibility remains only as potential risk. Numerous experiments have not shown even a single case of a bacterium picking up the marker gene from the plants. Furthermore, it is well know that the bacteria-antibiotic relationship is, in fact, much more complicated. First, any such risk as described above adds only a little more to the already existing risk. Many naturally occurring bacterial strains are already known to be resistant to ampicillin. Second, the behavior of the antibiotic resistant genes is by no means ironclad. Third, there are many other antibiotics which are quite effective against bacteria that are resistant to ampicillin. These arguments have convinced the North American regulators to approve the sale of the maize produced by the Ciba scientists.

We should also take into consideration various related concerns of the EU, such as economic and agri-business competition, and the traditional European concerns regarding the new food technologies which are widely used in the North American continent. For instance, American beef, which is produced with the aid of growth hormones, is banned in Europe. In these matters, European populations generally tend to be far more conservative and less willing to take new risks as the Americans have been.

8 Intellectual property rights and plant genetic resources

Following the Uruguay Round of negotiations, the countries of the developing world have come to realize increasingly that they must adopt the laws and regulations pertaining to intellectual property rights–a notion that is essentially conceived in the industrialized countries. The traditional property systems and conventional practices are being replaced by laws of international agreements which are designed in western countries. Consequently, this has resulted in much apprehension and economic uncertainty with regard to the future status of international trade as well as the continued enjoyment of local bio-resources which was taken for granted by people of the developing nations. They have become painfully aware that the sovereignty of their local biological resources is no longer guaranteed. There is also the general realization that the traditional intellectual properties in the developing nations, such as the farming practices which have conserved the crop germplasm for centuries and the medicinal applications of various plant derivatives, are not recognized or included in the intellectual property laws which are designed in the western countries. They have further become aware that western multinational companies are filing patents to stake claims on processes and products which have already been well recognized in the developing world for centuries, the only difference being the western products may have been produced by different methods.

The commercial exploitation of the intellectual property (and physical property as well) of the developing world involves a lopsided process that invariably results in the flow of bio-resources from the developing world to the industrialized nations. And, the economic benefits that result from this process are largely accrued by the industrialized nations, the developing nations receiving only a small fraction of the pie.

In addition to the problem of immediate economic exploitation there is also the obvious long-term destruction of third world biodiversity which invariably follows such lopsided exploitation. It is well know that various tropical species are becoming extinct each year and this extinction is far more rapid in the tropics than in the temperate regions of the world. It is further evident that the destruction of tropical forests and biodiversity spells doom not only for the developing nations but for the entire world as well.

It has been suggested by several authors and community activists that a diverse system of intellectual property rights, one which respects the rights of traditional cultures, is sorely needed.

These issues are discussed below with some recent examples of economic exploitation of third world bio-resources.

The impact of intellectual property rights is no where more obvious than in the whole range of issues related to plant genetic resources and crop resources. This subject has been the topic of discussion in numerous international conferences in recent years. The importance and value of genetic resources has been well recognized worldwide. The World Resources Institute (WRI) has termed the biochemical and genetic resources the "oil of the information age". Among the issues which are being debated are the North-South dialogue in sharing world's natural resources, ownership of intellectual property, and compensation for indigenous technologies as well as farmer's rights.

In the years following World War II, many nations began to lower their trade and tariff barriers to make them more open and permeable for international trade under the auspices of the General Agreement on Trade and Tariffs (GATT). Multilateral negotiations have been taking place, for instance, the Kennedy Round in the 1960s, the Tokyo Round in the 1970s, and more recently the Uruguay Round (which was formally signed in April, 1994), have all aimed at reducing border barriers and restrictions. The Uruguay Round was marked by an active participation by developing countries, for the first time in GATT negotiations.

There were certain consequences which resulted from the Uruguay Round negotiations. One important development is the stipulation that all signatories should adopt trade-related intellectual property rights protection (TRIPs). Another important development was the insistence by the governments of the developed countries that certain conditions required by the governments of the developing countries for investment by domestic and foreign firms such as the inclusion of local components, links between imports and exports, and export targets, etc. should be liberalized (TRIMs or trade-related investment measures). Another development of the Uruguay Round was to achieve agreement that trade in services would be brought under multilateral trade disciplines in the World Trade Organization (WTO).

In this context, it is well to emphasize that no one has been more eloquent in emphasizing the farmer's rights and intellectual property rights in the developing world than Prof. M.S. Swaminathan (1995). Through numerous publications, conferences, lectures and as Chairman of the United Nations' Committee on Intellectual Property Rights, Prof. Swaminathan has been making valuable contributions for the development of a fair and equitable world policy on intellectual property rights. Of special interest is the conference volume edited by Prof. Swaminathan, *Farmer's Rights and Plant Genetic Resources* (1995) which presents a most helpful dialogue on how the benefits of biodiversity and biotechnology can reach the "unreached." As he aptly states in his introduction:

> Apart from the Government of India, I'm sure the other developing countries, and other nations are also seized of the same problem which has assumed urgency after the conclusion of the Uruguay Round of GATT Negotiations and also after the coming into operation of the Biodiversity Convention.... Many people who discuss this matter do not appreciate the differences between us (India) and industrialized countries where framing is today really agribusiness. Each farm may be about 1000 hectares. Here it is one hectare or below in the case of most farms; hence, there is need for achieving a proper match between legislation and real life conditions. One has to apply one's mind to India's own situation.

The valuable contributions of Prof. Swaminathan and the Foundation that he established in Madras, India, are discussed on other pages.

Commercial exploitations of biodiversity in the developing countries has received a great deal of attention in recent years. Multinational companies from Europe and the United States have laid claims to various commercial products (including several of medicinal and pharmaceutical importance) which have been developed from the indigenous plant and animal species of the developing nations of Asia, Africa and South America.

Exploitation of biodiversity resources of the developing nations by individuals, groups and companies which are not a part of these communities and are remotely placed in distinct geographic regions, their only interest being financial windfalls, inherently carries with it the same mental attitude as the old empires exhibited towards their colonial territories. Technology places far more power in the hands of a few industrialized countries as compared to the great majority of humanity. The immediate effect of implementing intellectual property rights today is to widen the gap between the rich and the poor nations. Poor countries will have to pay more for certain goods, some of which were developed from naturally occurring species in their own backyard, and industrialized nations will be the beneficiaries. Economic disparity between these two groups of nations will increase. Impoverished communities worldwide lack the economic strength and trained personnel to protect their natural resources against the predatory exploitations of multinational companies. They are easy prey to unscrupulous corporations.

Farmer's Rights

As mentioned earlier, in recent years Prof. M.S. Swaminathan (1995) eloquently advocated the concept of Farmer's Rights. He proposed a draft legislation relating to plant breeders' and farmers' rights, an act of legislation titled "Plant Variety Recognition and Rights Act", with the following aims:

> The first is . . . to promote conservation and evaluation and sustainable utilization of plant genetic resources,
> Secondly, to revive and strengthen the in situ conservation of landraces and folk varieties, which are the results of a thousand years of natural and human selection,
> Thirdly, to impart the pro-nature, pro-poor and pro-women orientation in plant breeding seed technology,
> Fourthly, to endure the genetic resources utilized in an effective and equitable manner to strengthen the food security of the nation and the livelihood security of the ecologically, economically and socially underprivileged sections of society, and finally, to bring to the people of India the benefits of modern technology . . . through greater investment both in technology development and genetic conservation.

Among several significant suggestions made by Prof. Swaminathan are the creation of a National Bureau of Forest Genetic Resources and also a National Institute of Plant Variety Testing and Evaluation. Although these suggestions are made with special reference to India, they are applicable to all developing countries.

The issues of intellectual property rights and plant genetic resources as they apply to medicinal plants is discussed in detail in Chapter 9.

Table 8.1 Human behavior and social changes affecting biological diversity

Up to 1500 A.D.	
• Domestication of plants and animals	• International trade (both by land and sea)
• Hunting and gathering	• Expansion of empires and wars
• Fire	• Population movements (mass migrations)
• Agriculture	• Market economics (Asia, Middle East)

1500 to 1900 A.D.	
• Large scale migrations	• Appreciation of diverse species through botanical gardens and zoos, and promoting international trade
• European domination of Asia, Africa and South America	
• Strengthening market economies by establishing stock exchanges in London and Amsterdam	• Slavery in Africa and increased hunting in Asia and Africa
• Changing food habits and import patterns (spices, coffee, tea, chocolate, sugar, rice, etc.)	

1900 to 2000 A.D.	
• Invention of air travel and vacation packages to remote lands (Galapagos, Malaysia, Africa, etc.), television programs	• World wars and population displacements
	• Large scale chemical and biological pollution
• Construction of large scale hydro-electric and other energy producing projects	• Open air testing of nuclear weapons
	• Agribusiness and multinationals, focus on cash crops
• Mining, mechanized fishing of oceans	• Biological patents and intellectual property rights
• Rapid population expansion and greater demand for housing	

Source: Modified after McNealy (1995)

Table 8.2 Wildlife habitat loss by conversion: Asia and Africa

Country*	Original Wildlife Habitat	Remaining Habitat	% Loss
Bangladesh	1,142,777	68,567	94
Hong Kong	1,066	32	97
India	3,017,009	615,095	80
Sri Lanka	64,700	10,999	83
Vietnam	332,116	66,423	80
Kampuchea	180,879	43,411	76
Pakistan	165,900	39,816	76
Philippines	308,211	64,724	79
Burkina Faso	273,800	54,760	80
Burundi	25,700	3,598	86
Gambia	11,300	1,243	89
Ghana	230,000	46,000	80
Liberia	111,400	14,482	87
Chad	720,800	172,992	76
Cote d'Ivoire	318,000	66,780	79
Madagascar	595,211	148,803	75
Mauritania	388,600	73,834	81
Rwanda	25,100	3,263	87
Senegal	196,200	35,316	82
Sierra Leone	71,700	10,755	85

*Only those with 75% loss or higher are included.

Source: McNeely, 1995

Table 8.3 Diminishing Bird Populations in Great Britain (1970-1988)

Bird Species	% of decline
Corn Bunting	69
Gray Partridge	67
Tree Sparrow	67
Lapwing	59
Bullfinch	58
Song Thrush	54
Turtle Dove	48
Linnet	36
Skylark	33
Spotted Flycatcher	31
Blackbird	28

Source: Fuller et al, 1991

Table 8.4 Desertification of world's rangelands within the drylands (in thousands of hectares)

Region	Under desertification	% Desertified
Asia	995, 080	74.0
Africa	1, 187, 610	75.0
Australia	361, 350	55.0
Europe	80, 517	72.0
N. America	411, 154	75.0
S. America	297, 754	76.0

A PBR system for India

Swaminathan (1995) and others have emphasized that the trend which is increasingly becoming more common in the western countries towards large scale agri-business would be dangerous for India where 25 percent of the world's farmers cultivate land. Most of them are quite poor, their land holdings being very small–75 percent of the farming families have less than 2 hectares per family. However, in some respects, the situation in India is quite similar to that of Canada and Australia: large government financed plant breeding programs, a strong federal constitution but the States being quite autonomous in the matter of agricultural legislation. However, there is one important difference. In India, over 70 percent of the population depends on agriculture for their livelihood (Swaminathan, 1995). Any legislation must take into account how it might impact on this large population from the viewpoint of not only food production, but also economics, equity and employment. Of special importance are women because they play a pivotal role in agricultural practices such as seed selection and propagation.

With reference to farmers' rights in India, Swaminathan (1995) had emphasized that the contributions from families in the selection and conservation of plant genetic resources should be recognized. It has been emphasized that for certain crops such as rice, farmers from several countries may be involved in developing the landraces.

It is difficult to reconcile both national legislation for Farmer's rights and international agreements which would be agreeable to all nations under one umbrella. The latter comes more appropriately under the responsibility of such international bodies as the UPOV and FAO, etc. Dr. Swaminathan had drafted the very first PBR legislation for India. However, he also pointed out that the "procedures must be simple, direct, transparent and just, if enormous litigation is to be avoided. If this is not accomplished, both farmers and breeders will suffer". With reference to possible agreement at the international level, Swaminathan (1995) stated that:

> The ultimate aim should be to convert UPOV into an International Union which will help to protect both farmers' and breeders' rights. Charity begins at home and hence we should first show the way to the world how to fulfill our obligations to farm and tribal women and men.

The primary goals of the legislation are to promote conservation and sustainable use of plant genetic resources, to revive the in situ conservation of landraces and folk varieties, to impart the pro-nature, pro-poor and pro-women orientation in plant breeding and seed technology, to strengthen the food security of the nation and the livelihood security of the farming families, and to bring to the people of India the benefits of modern technology (Swaminathan, 1995). Surely such a program would be an ideal goal for all developing nations!

Plant variety protection in a developing country

A leading world renowned center in biotechnology is the M.S. Swaminathan Research Foundation in Madras, India. Under the leadership of Prof. Swaminathan, a series of conferences and symposia have focused attention, in recent years, on the issue of intellectual property rights (IPR) with special reference to plant breeders' rights and plant variety protection. In a preface to a recent conference that was held in January, 1996, Swaminathan wrote:

> The future of global food security depends on the success of our efforts in the conservation and enhancement of agrobiodiversity.... Agrobiodiversity is not evenly distributed over the globe and tends to be more concentrated in the tropical and sub-tropical regions of the world.... The proceedings will show that the long term conservation of agrobiodiversity will become feasible only if the concept of Farmer's Rights becomes an operational reality.

Thus, in a few words, Swaminathan (1996) laid the foundation for preserving global plant genetic resources. Future of global food security is closely tied to the conservation of agrobiodiversity which is more concentrated in the tropics and sub-tropics and which depends on the realization of Farmer's Rights.

In the same conference, C.S. Srinivasan summarized the present status of plant variety protection in India (1996). Intellectual Property Rights are governed by the Indian Patents Act of 1970. However, life forms have not been covered under the Indian Patents Act. There are several reasons for strengthening the plant variety protection: (a) PVP system will encourage private sector investment to sustain high quality plant breeding research; (b) most countries have organized their PBR (Plant Breeders' Rights) legislation on a principle of reciprocity. PVP will enable Indian breeders to benefit from the protection afforded by this arrangement; (c) A large number of countries have already established a system of PBR, and if India does not have a system of protection of its own, the access of Indian farmers to plant genetic resources of other countries would be restricted; (d) PBR will ensure India's access to world markets involving agricultural exports, etc.

Some related concerns are that PBR may accelerate the process of erosion of agrobiodiversity, may increase dependence on foreign and expensive sources of supply, and may weaken public funding for research and development.

Farmer's Rights are conceived as an integral part of the legislation rather than as an issue that is secondary to a system of Plant Breeder's Rights. Under the TRIPS agreement, micro-organisms should also be included under the patenting system and this matter is under further discussion as to the best way of including it under the PVP legislation.

Plant Breeders' Rights in Latin America

Plant breeders' rights legislation has been recently introduced in five Latin American countries, including Argentina, Chile, Colombia, Mexico, and Uruguay. One of the main reasons to introduce PBR in Latin America was to improve the transfer of foreign plant breeding technology to domestic plant breeders, seed propagators, and growers, by assuring foreign breeders that their varieties would enjoy legal protection against unauthorized use. This subject has been recently review by Van Wijk and Jaffe (1996), and was partly based on a survey conducted in 1994 by the Inter-American Institute for Cooperation on Agriculture (IICA) and the University of Amsterdam (UA). The seed industry was strong enough only in Argentina, Chile, and Uruguay to enact PBR.

A proposal to establish legal protection for plant varieties was submitted to the Argentine Congress in 1936 by a ministerial ad hoc commission. However, that bill was never discussed, and it was forty years later that PBR was introduced in Argentina because of lobbying by some influential breeders. In Chile, PBR protection was promulgated in 1977 in response to demands of domestic and foreign seed companies. In Uruguay, the first steps in plant variety protection were initiated in the mid-1970s, by Shell Oil Company, which was involved in seed activities in that country. Those efforts were supported by multinational seed companies. Uruguay's close trade-ties to Argentina also provided incentives. PBR legislation was enacted in 1981 and was modified and regulated in 1984 by various bylaws. In Argentina, Chile, and Uruguay, PBR was only of limited success because of limited enforcement. However, the protection was strengthened in all three countries in 1994, to harmonize with international standards.

Conflict over insufficient legal protection for advanced technology in Mexico has been a source of continuing friction between the Mexican and the U.S. Governments. Mexico began to strengthen its IPR in 1990 when plans for the North American Free Trade Agreement (NAFTA) began to take shape. Mexico was expected to adopt PBR legislation by the end of 1994. However, the PBR bill, the *Ley Federal del Derecho del Creador de Variedades Vegetales*, continued to be discussed long afterwards. Much of the opposition to the adoption of a PBR system in Mexico came from the public sector. Greater antipathy toward privatization of public sector research was expressed by the Mexican breeders and researchers in the public sector. Farmers' associations and non-governmental organizations (NGOs) that are associated with small-scale farmers are among such groups. Protection of plant varieties under the industrial patent law came under dispute by the promulgation of a new patent law in 1991. However, the patent law itself was amended in 1994 and does not provide protection for plant varieties any longer. Plant varieties are now protected under PBR legislation.

With respect to Colombia, PBR protection was introduced when the Andean Pact countries decided to establish a common regime on PBR. In October, 1993, the Junta of the Cartagena Agreement adopted a decision which was based on the draft PBR law proposed to the Colombian Senate. A second decision enabled the protection of plant material, plants, or plant varieties under patent law. The question of PBR was hotly debated among seed companies, public institutes, NGOs, and government departments. Advocates of PBR include Acosemillas, an association of Colombian and foreign seed companies; ICA, the main public agricultural research center; the Ministry of Agriculture; and Ascolflores, the association of cut flower producers and exporters. Domestic demands for PBR were supported by the U.S Government for stronger intellectual property protection. As in Mexico, opposition to PBR came from the academic community, indigenous groups, several agricultural NGOs, and the Ministry of Environment. Their main concern was that the PBR may harm local farmers and diminish biodiversity.

All four countries–Argentina, Uruguay, Mexico and Colombia–are in step with the convention of the International Union for the Protection of New Varieties of Plants (UPOV). All have committed to providing for legal protection of plant varieties under the new multilateral trade agreement under GATT. Germplasm and related information is generally freely available at the international agricultural research centers (IARCs). Two such centers are located in Latin America; the International Center for Tropical Agriculture (CIAT) in Colombia and the

International Center for the Improvement of Maize and Wheat (CIMMYT) in Mexico. These centers protect improved material when required but do not generally seek intellectual property protection for their materials. They keep their germplasm in the public domain. However, certain material transfer agreements must be concluded for any exploitation of the germplasm. The germplasm generated by the CIMMYT is available to others provided its protection is compatible with the center's policies. CIAT also freely offers its materials provided the receivers inform CIAT about its use and do not attempt to protect a material outside the country of its origin. For instance, a company in Mexico may protect a CIAT-derived material in Mexico, but not elsewhere (van Wijk and Jaffe, 1996).

Related issues include access to germplasm from private companies in OECD countries, especially for advanced breeding lines of hybrid grains and vegetables as well as the germplasm of fruit and cut flowers. In the absence of PBR protection, foreign growers and companies provided materials to Latin Americans under gentlemen's agreements and contract laws. However, it is that access to foreign breeding line and ornamental and fruit varieties will improve significantly with an operative PBR system in place. For their part, the Latin American countries are revising their export policies to protect the germplasm of such tropical crops as cacao, coffee, tea, oil palm, and sugar cane, for commercial exploitation.

Another issue is protection for essentially derived varieties. Under the 1991 UPOV act, it was possible to make a small change in an existing variety and to protect the new variety under PBR, with no obligation to original breeder. In Colombia and Mexico, the PBR laws include provisions for essentially derived varieties, but in Uruguay, Argentina, and Chile, they do not provide such protection. A new law proposed in Mexico requires that permission of the original breeder is necessary if the new variety possesses identifiable characteristics of an existing variety. The PBR legislation in Latin America (as elsewhere) enables the breeder, for a period about 15 to 20 years, to propagate and control material at will, to propagate essentially derived material, and to market the harvest grown from that variety.

Patenting of animals

Following precedent opinions by the supreme court and PTO Board of Appeals, the U.S. Patent and Trademark Office (PTO) Board of Appeals and Interferences, announced in 1987 that "nonnaturally occurring nonhuman multicellular living

Table 8.5 PBR in five Latin American countries (1995)

Country	Adoption and regulation	Effective Enforcement	Accession to UPOV
Argentina	1973/78	1990	1994
Chile	1977 (modified 1994)	1994	1995
Colombia	1993/94	–	1995
Mexico	1995	–	1995
Uruguay	1984/87	1994	1994

Source: Van Wijk and Jaffe, 1996

organisms, including animals, to be patentable subject". The Board further stated that its "decision does not affect the principle and practice that products found in nature will not be considered to be patentable subject matter ... unless given a new form, quality, properties, or combination not present in the original article existing in nature in accordance with existing law".

With respect to the patenting of human beings, the Board stated that:

> A claim will not be considered to be patentable subject matter ... the Patent and Trademark Office is now examining claims directed to multicellular living organism, including animals. To the extent that the claimed subject matter is directed to a nonhuman 'nonnaturally occurring manufacture or composition of matter–a product of human ingenuity' (Diamond v. Chakrabarty), such claims will not be rejected under 35 U.S.C. 101 as being directed to nonstatutory subject matter.

U.S. federal regulation

In the United States, several federal agencies are involved in regulating the use of genetically modified animals in research and product development. These are:

(1) U.S. Patent and Trademark Office (USPTO),
(2) U.S. Department of Agriculture (including Agricultural Research Service, Animal and Plant Health Inspection Service, Cooperative State

Research Service, Food Safety and Inspection Service, and Office of Agriculture Biotechnology),
(3) Food and Drug Administration (FDA),
(4) Environmental Protection Agency (EPA),
(5) National Science Foundation (NSF),
(6) National Institutes of Health (NIH),
(7) Alcohol, Drug Abuse, and Mental Health Administration (ADAMHA),
(8) Agency for International Development (AID),
(9) Department of Interior (Fish and Wildlife Service),
(10) National Aeronautics and Space Administration (NASA), and
(11) Department of Energy.

The above list underlines the growing importance of biotechnology and especially the importance of genetic modification in research and development.

9 Conservation of medicinal plants

The world's genetic resources have been steadily declining over the last few centuries. It has been estimated that during the years 1600 and 1900, about 75 species of plants and animals became extinct. However, the pace of extinction picked up and about the same number became extinct since 1900. Predictions of future extinctions are so extreme that these past extinctions pale by comparison. The International Union for the conservation of Nature (IUCN) and the World Wildlife Fund (WWF) estimated that 60,000 higher plant species could become extinct by the middle of the next century unless adequate conservation measures are implemented to reverse the present trend.

The threat of extinction is even more realistic when considering the exploitation of medicinal plants. The world demand for pharmaceuticals has been going up steadily. An estimate by geographic region is presented. It is further estimated that drugs containing one or more plant-derived active ingredients represented about 25 percent of all prescriptions dispensed from community pharmacies in the United States. But, the estimates vary from country to country. In Eastern Europe, the proportion of prescriptions containing plant drugs is more than 60 percent because traditional medicine and modern medicine are amalgamated. The corresponding figure in Chinese system of medicine is more than 80 percent. Both the Indian traditional system and the Chinese system use more than 200 species of plants in their pharmacopoeias. Some commonly used medicinal plants and their pharmacological uses are listed in Table 9.3.

NCI-sponsored collections of medicinal plants

The major objective of the plant exploration program is to collect plants for anticancer and anti-HIV evaluation. The countries covered in Asia included Indonesia, Philippines, Malaysia, Papua New Guinea, Thailand, Taiwan, Nepal, Pakistan, and China.

During the first five-year cycle, which was completed in 1991, thirty-five botanical experiments, primarily in Southeast Asia, were undertaken under a contract with the National Cancer Institute (NCI), an agency of the United States government headquartered in Bethesda, Maryland. Most of the team members were from the faculty of the college of Pharmacy, University of Illinois in Chicago (Soejarto et al, 1996). During that period, more than 10,000 samples belonging to 2,000 species were collected. The breakdown of plant parts is as follows:

Plant part	% of the samples
Leaves and twigs	51.0
Stem	21.0
Flowers, fruits, and seeds	17.0
Roots	9.0
Whole plants	2.0

A high volume of sample collection was made in the Philippines, Indonesia, Malaysia, and Papua New Guinea. The investigators considered that their work demonstrated the medicinal value of their forest resources to the host country. Of course, the indigenous people of those regions have already been aware of this fact. Now they have additional information from a different perspective.

During the initial five years of the expeditionary work, about 3,000 samples were collected in the Philippines. These have been screened for anti-cancer and anti-AIDS evaluation. The island of Palawan received much of the attention because of its extremely rich flora; 1,700 species of flowering plants in an area of 1.2 million hectares!

The Malay Peninsula is another rich source; 7,500 flowering plant species, of which about 3,000 are tree species, and in Borneo the total estimate is 10,000 to 15,000 species. Three collecting expeditions to Sarawak and Sabah resulted in a total of 964 collections, which included 2,203 samples.

In the entire island of New Guinea, there are at least 9,000 flowering plant species, of which about 90 percent may be endemic (Good, 1960). In Papua New Guinea itself, the forest cover is estimated to be about 85 percent (Davis et al, 1986). Two long-term residency expeditions were made under the sponsorship of the NCI in 1988 and 1989, and two more shorter expeditions took place in 1990 and 1991. During the initial phase, 463 collections, comprising of 1,511 samples were collected.

Thailand

About 12,000 flowering plant species are found in Thailand. Only one NCI-sponsored collecting trip was made (in 1987). A total of 265 collections, and 469 samples were collected. Although only one trip was made to Thailand, it was found to be one of the richest sources for taxonomic diversity (Soejarto et al, 1996). Evergreen tropical rain forests, dry evergreen and deciduous dipterocarp forests, deciduous teak forests, mixed deciduous forests, and mangrove forests abound in Thailand.

Taiwan

Despite its small size Taiwan has a rich flora, which includes different types ranging from low-saturated evergreen tropical rain forests to mixed and coniferous forests and grasslands above 1,800 m. The number of flowering plant species is about 3,000. A short collecting trip was sponsored by the NCI in 1989 which produced 43 collections and 68 samples of high taxonomic diversity. The collection showed some overlap with the endemics from southern (tropical) China (Soejarto, 1996).

Nepal

The vegetation ranges from tropical evergreen forest in the valleys to alpine meadows at higher elevations, comprising of some 6,500 flowering species. But only about 5 percent are estimated to be endemic. A single NCI-supported expedition from Yale University in 1987 resulted in 33 collections and 103 samples with special types of information about their indigenous medical use. Their samples were used for anti-HIV test screenings.

Balochistan (Pakistan)

The area bordering Iran is mostly semi-desert and desert with tropical thorn scrubs. A single NCI-supported ethnobotanical expedition by the Field Museum of Natural

History in 1990, netted 1,000 collections, of which 200 were collected, producing some 46 samples for the NCI program.

Indonesia

Indonesia provided one of the richest sources for plant species; over 10,000 tree species and at least 15,000 flowering plant species. Initially, seven major expeditions were undertaken by the University of Illinois–Harvard team in cooperation with the Bogor Herbarium in Indonesia. Another botanical collecting expedition–a small ethnopharmocology project–was funded by the WWF, jointly with three of the NCI-sponsored expeditions in 1988 and 1989. Local botanists of the Herbarium Bogoriense in Bogor, a part of the Division of the Council for Sciences of Indonesia, offered much assistance as their collaborators. It is not clear, however, if an agreement pertaining to the sharing of intellectual property rights has been signed by the Indonesian authorities as required by the GATT regulations.

In a broader context, it is not clear, however, if the intellectual property rights of the indigenous people have been honored in an appropriate manner according to the GATT regulations. Such facts are usually not mentioned in scientific publications. And it is not clear either if any formal contracts have been signed with the local communities or various governments to share any potential financial windfalls which may result as a consequence of research involving these plant materials. Should NCI enter into a contract with a pharmaceutical company for specific drug development it is also not clear if the indigenous populations would enjoy a similar partnership and receive a fair share of the financial benefits. One can hardly imagine that an unsophisticated and poorly educated tribal population, who have already been using these plants for centuries for medicinal purposes, would have the knowledge and foresight to claim intellectual property rights. The basic question is: Who owns the intellectual property that has been around for centuries?

Soejarto et al (1996) stated that during the second cycle of the plant collection program (1991-1996), the National Cancer Institute (NCI-NIH) provided a letter of agreement to strengthen any pledge to return a share of possible future monetary benefits to the country of collection. But no details are provided and it is not clear if the countries of collection are satisfied with this agreement. It is also not clear if the indigenous and tribal people who have been directly responsible for preserving the intellectual property will eventually receive any part of the economic benefits when they become available.

Several authors in recent years have discussed the problem of intellectual property rights with special reference to developing countries. Khalil (1995) reviewed this problem with special reference to the conservation of medicinal plants in the developing world. He wrote:

> The new medicinal plant varieties, or the genes responsible for therapy, may increasingly become the focus of patent protection in the years ahead. At the same time, the rights and roles of the indigenous communities in conserving plant genetic resources. For most forest communities, the use of medicinal plants carry no rights of the kind conceived of in industrialized countries.

A common practice cited by Khalil involves the screening of medicinal plants by foreign expeditionary forces. These forces are often sent by multinational companies. These forces are invariably assisted by the local tribal communities who are easily lured by a few dollars. It is not widely realized that such screening expeditions and the ensuing exploitation often lead to the extinction of several medicinal species. Diminishing range of medicinal plant species creates not only an export problem but also adversely affects the primary health care system of the indigenous communities for whom these plant species often represent the only remedy available. The problem is, in fact, made much worse because of wastage through poor packaging methods as well as limited shelf-life of the raw materials that are being exported.

The danger of overexploitation was evident in the case of two medicinal plants from Africa, one from Ghana and the other from Cameroon. The bark of the plant *Khaya senegalensis* is very much in demand in Ghana for gum and herbal remedies. In Cameroon, the plant *Pygeum africanus* is used for treating problems of the urinary tract. Both have become endangered species (Heywood, 1994). The Cameroon government started a program of gradual debarking to conserve the species. There are no systematic studies of the supply and demand dynamics and no program of control in most parts of Africa.

Three other cases of exploitation were cited by Khalil (1995). He wrote: "We are witnessing a rising tide of anger because for too long products developed, cultivated and conserved through generations of selective interbreeding are being appropriated in the name of foreigners". In one instance, an American university has applied for a patent on endod, a berry-producing plant found in Ethiopia which is believed to have fungicidal properties. But the indigenous people of Ethiopia are not among the beneficiaries. As the regenerative capacity of the plant falls short of its demand there is a real danger of genetic erosion. The second case is a plant found in Kenya, *Maytenus buchanii*, which is used by the indigenous Digo community for treating cancer. The NCI took the whole stock for research purposes; however, the Digo community's rights were not recognized. Another plant—the rosy periwinkle, a native of Madagascar and Jamaica—is now cultivated extensively in the U.S. It is the source of two anticancerous drugs, vincristine and vinblastine, but the indigenous communities of Madagascar and Jamaica who conserved this plant for centuries have received no compensation.

A similar situation prevails in another part of the world, Indonesia. A plant called *gaharu* has been used traditionally for treating complications of pregnancy and childbirth in several countries of southeast Asia. However, its distribution is sparse and it has a low regenerative quality. Consequently, the supply is uneven and the price fluctuates frequently. Because of its poor conservation and high demand, *gaharu* is almost extinct in many areas where it was once available.

In contrast, in China there are very harsh laws against exploitation and destruction of medicinal plant species. A systematic conservation program specifies the manner of harvesting, stage of growth of plant, parts to be harvested, and the amounts harvested. Gene banks have been established to conserve germplasm of medicinal plants and most widely consumed species are being cultivated (Pei-gen, 1991). The Institute of Medicinal Plant Development (IMPLAD) is a WHO collaborating Center of Traditional Medicine in Beijing, which specializes in the research of medicinal plants under the auspices of the Chinese Academy of Medical Sciences (CAMS).

Factors affecting biodiversity

It is an undeniable fact that encroaching human populations and larger numbers of domestic animals have led to the diminishing forest areas and wild life habitats which, in turn, has narrowed the range of biodiversity quite significantly. McNeely, Gadgil and others (1995) have discussed this problem in detail, and I have summarized their work along with information from other sources.

The most frequent cause for loss of biodiversity is habitat destruction. Human impact results in either conversion of one habitat type to another or modification of conditions within a habitat. Human population expansion, poor agricultural practices, fires, erosion, animal grazing, and economic exploitation by multinationals with no sensible conservation plan often result in habitat loss. Transfer of technology should go hand-in-hand with appropriate conservation measures. As an indicator of global biodiversity loss, Meyer and Turner (1992) presented the following data on human-induced land conversion.

Type of Land	Percent Changed
Cropland	+ 543.0
Irrigated Cropland	+ 2400.0
Closed Forest	- 15.1
Forest and Woodland	- 14.9
Grassland/Pasture	- 1.0

Forest land is the richest repository for biodiversity. In the tropics, this is even more intense. Habitat loss through conversion has impacted on certain countries of the developing world much more intensely than others. It is not surprising that there is a high correlation with counties of high population density. Hong Kong and Bangladesh, which possess the highest population densities in the world, also indicate the highest habitat loss. Hannah et al (1994) showed that 73 percent of the world's land surface other than rock, ice, and barren land is either human-dominated (36 percent) or partially disturbed (37 percent), and 27 percent is undisturbed. However, no part of the world can be considered truly "undisturbed".

In many parts of the world loss of biodiversity is due to desertification under excessive human pressure. A recent UN conference on desertification estimated that 6 percent of the world's area to be "man-made deserts". About a quarter of the world's surface area is estimated to be threatened by desertification. It is interesting that, with the exception of Australia, there appears to be a general agreement on the percentage of rangeland desertified.

Medicinal Plants of India

It is well known that India is a rich source of medicinal plants and that it has a long tradition of indigenous medicine (*Ayurveda*). The best known of these is the *neem* tree which is widely used for dental hygiene and also as a pesticide. According to Sundaresh (1982), the total value of medicinal exports of India exceeds $50 million dollars per year. This estimate is based on earlier figures and the current value is undoubtedly much higher. Table 9.4 gives a list of some of the major medicinal exports of India.

The National Cancer Institute (NIH)

The growing demand for developing medicinal products from the plant species of the developing world is illustrated by the research program of the National Cancer Institute (NCI) of the National Institutes of Health (NIH) in the United States. The National Cancer Institute awarded three five-year contracts, in September 1986, for collections of plants in tropical and subtropical regions worldwide. The three contractors are as follows:

Collector	Collection Region
(1) Missouri Botanical Garden	Tropical and Sub-tropical regions of Africa, Madagascar and neighboring islands
(2) New York Botanical Garden	Central and South America (rain forest regions)
(3) University of Illinois at Chicago; Arnold Arboretum at Harvard; and the Bishop Museum at Honolulu	Southeast Asia

Each contractee was assigned the task of collecting 1500 samples of 0.3-1.0 kg (dry weight) per year. Collections may include branches, roots, flowers, leaves, and bark, etc. In addition to the NCI samples, each species is represented by a sample placed in the Smithsonian Museum of Natural History (Botany Department) which can be referred for re-collections when necessary. At least 50,000 specimens had been collected in the following years.

The conservation challenge

Soejarto et al (1996) discussed the problem of conserving these plant species for posterity. They wrote:

A challenge to be faced in collecting plants for anticancer and anti-HIV evaluation is the performance of the collection work without endangering the environment and/or the species collected. Our plant-collecting practices have been developed with this conservation challenge in mind; minimal disturbance to the forest habitat was given a high priority in the collection process. This was achieved primarily by using tree climbers to collect the aerial parts of a tree, by making a narrow longitudinal strip cut on one side of a tree in collecting the stembark, by tracing the root to a distance (2-3 m) from the tree base in collecting the root, by leaving a collecting site in the same condition as it was found, and by extinguishing all campfires completely.

Some aspects of property rights

Legally speaking, a "property" is something in which an individual or legal entity can assert rights against others. Intellectual property rights are a specific form of property law which protects the products of man's creativity (Walden, 1995). Land ownership usually confers a set of rights on the owner, such as any valuable mineral wealth contained within the earth or a natural genetic material discovered on the land that may have medicinal or some other practical applications. The land owner then has the exclusive rights to harvest and market the products. This basic right is recognized in the Rio Biodiversity convention, Article 15, "Access to Genetic Resource":

> 1. Recognizing the sovereign rights of States over their natural resources, the authority to determine access to genetic resources rests with the national governments and is subject to national legislation.

In response, some governments, such as that of the State of Queensland (Australia), proposed an amendment to its Nature Conservation Act, "to give the state outright ownership of its flora and fauna and guarantee that it shares in any profits made from exploiting them". Such legislation was meant to halt any systematic exploitation by foreign companies and laboratories.

INBio and Merck agreement

The government of Costa Rica established a research organization to help identify and inventory Costa Rica's biodiversity and to integrate its nondestructive use into the intellectual and economic fabric of the society. Thus biodiversity conservation becomes a central feature of all sectors of the society. It provides employment for rural people as "parataxonomists". The information generated by the institute has many uses including chemical screening, and in collaboration with Merck & Co., pharmaceutical development and new product development.

Merck & Co. paid $1.1 million in advance in exchange for samples of high quality. This is ten times the traditional service payment. Reid et al (1996) reviewed the nature of company-collector contracts. Conservation, development, and equity are among the provisions which are included in such contracts. All INBio commercial contracts specify that a portion of the research and royalty budget goes directly to the National Park Fund at the Ministry of Natural Resources, Energy and Mines, and for other wildland conservation measures.

Who owns biodiversity?

A fundamental question is concerned with the legitimacy of extending intellectual property rights to wild genetic and biochemical resources. Patenting of wild species would be impractical because patent offices would be overwhelmed by speculative claims on species with no known utility. Furthermore, it would enable the private ownership to appropriate large sections of the "public domain" to an extent which would be detrimental to public interests. However, IPR can stimulate domestic innovation and technology transfer, thus stimulating further sustainable development within the source country.

The INBio-Merck contract is not exclusive; both parties are free to trade with other organizations. There is a stipulation, however, that INBio will not send the same sample to a competing company for a period of six months to two years. Economic returns resulting from biodiversity can be used for conserving the resource. Additional returns can be earned by a biodiversity-prospecting institution by selling information obtained through preliminary screening of samples for their biological and chemical properties. The potential value of such information would attract prospective contractees who would be interested in developing the products further.

The question of compensation for the holders of traditional knowledge such as farmers or practitioners of indigenous medicine was discussed by several authors. For instance, Reid et al (1996) claimed that "traditional knowledge is rarely involved in the development of new pharmaceutical products from biodiversity".They suggest, however, that farmers who have developed and protected the genetic and biochemical resources which are now being used may receive compensation through an international financial mechanism such as the Fund for Plant Genetic Resources or the convention on Biological diversity. Of course, this is nothing new. Swaminathan (1995) and others from the developing nations have repeatedly argued in favor of farmers' rights for many years. For instance, recent legislation in the Indian Parliament goes a long way in recognizing the rights of farmers. This topic is discussed in detail elsewhere in this book.

It is also arguable whether the modern science of natural products chemistry is entirely a new development with no connection whatsoever with past traditions. It is easy to show that chemistry evolved as a desire to put alchemy on a scientific footing. Traditional knowledge of herbal medicine and the pharmacopoeia, developed in different ancient cultures, played a significant role in developing the modern science of natural products chemistry. Tribal and indigenous healers recognized the medicinal value of certain plant species and are primarily responsible for propagating and protecting those species through centuries. Indeed, without those traditional conservation methods the modern prospecting expeditions by the U.S. National Cancer Institute would have been futile.

The same comment applies to the value of traditional farming practices. Traditional selection methods to propagate high yield and disease-resistant strains of various crops and the conservation of their germplasms are important forerunners to modern mechanized agriculture. A farmer cannot produce crops unless the germplasm of crops has been handed down through centuries. The question of seeking compensation for farmers and indigenous healers is discussed in detail elsewhere.

International agreements and national technology policies can further the interests of developing nations. Long term benefits and sustaining support for biodiversity can only come from domestic legislation which protects the sovereignty of intellectual property rights. IPR should be a useful tool to achieve this goal. However, many developing countries lack the necessary knowledge, trained personnel or even the minimum expenditure required to initiate an effective biodiversity program. The example of INBio illustrates how a small nation can use biodiversity to further its economic interests while protecting its sovereignty of intellectual property rights.

Table 9.1 Domestic regulation and international competition

Subject	Policy Instruments	Examples
IPR	Patent regulations	Biotechnology, pharmaceuticals
Technology policy	Government R & D support, public/private partnership	Human genome project, semiconductors
Environmental regulation	Conservation rules, FDA regulations, emission controls	Food crops, forestry, utilities, etc.
Standards	Product quality, health and safety	Biotechnology, computers, software
Foreign investment	Ownership limits, licensing and other technology transfer rules	Global manufacturing & service industries

Source: Doremus, 1995

Table 9.2 World demand for prescription drugs (1980 estimates)

Region	% of Total
U.S. & Canada	22.1
South America	6.5
Western Europe	31.0
Eastern Europe	11.7
East Asia	19.7
Central Asia	1.7
West Asia	2.1
Southeast Asia	1.6
Africa	3.0
Australasia	0.7

Source: Principe, 1991

Table 9.3 Some commonly used medicinal plants

Plant Species	Therapeutic Use
Dioscorea sp.	anti-inflammatory
Agave sp.	anti-arthritic
Solanum sp.	hormonal
Papaver somniferum	sedative
Cinchona	anti-malarial
Datura sp.	parasympatholytic
Digitalis lanata	cardiotonic
Rauvolfia sp.	hypotensive vasodilator
Catharanthus roseus	vasodilator anti-cancer
Camellia sinensis	CNS stimulant
Erythroylum coca	anaesthetic
Ehpedra sp.	sympathomimetic
Cephaelis ipecacuanha	anti-amoebic
Claviceps purpurea	oxytocic, vasoconstrictor vasodilator
Plantago ovata	laxative
Vinca minor	vasodilator
Glycorrhiza glabra	anti-inflammatory
Cassia sp.	laxative
Berberis sp.	anti-diarrheal

Source: Husain, 1991

Table 9.4 Medicinal exports of India

Product	Tons
Opium	2,132
Psyllium	29,910
Menthol	200
Cinchona alkaloids	50
Senna	3,800
Diosgenin	20
Srychnos alkaloids	16
Rauvolfia alkaloids	3
Ergot	16
Xanthotoxin	0.1
Berberine	3
Ipecac	20
Belladonna	28
Pyrethrum flowers	16

Source: I. Sundaresh, 1982

National Cancer Institute (NIH)

Equity in Biodiversity Utilization

Mays et al (1991) examined the problem of equitable compensation with reference to the utilization of traditional knowledge and biological materials from developing countries in commercial pharmaceutical production. The two questions posed by them are: (a) what constitutes equitable compensation of source countries and indigenous people in exchange for the utilization of their traditional knowledge and biological materials? and (b) how indigenous people and/or foreign governments should be compensated for the use of information and biomaterial? There is increasing concern that the world's patent laws may not be adequate to compensate source countries and indigenous people for their contributions. There is a new awareness of "equity", which may be defined as a fair and just treatment of a party. In natural-products drug discovery, quite often, the meaning of "equity" depends on the extent to which a developed country and a developing country can reach a common ground on its interpretation. The obvious beneficiaries include the public, those responsible for the identification and development of the compound, scientists who isolate the active compound from the natural product, and the commercial firm that obtains the patent rights to develop the final product. But, two important entities —source countries (which are usually developing countries providing natural products to facilitate drug discovery) and indigenous communities—are excluded from that group under the current patent law. Mays et al (1991) suggested that a contract offering future benefits may provide sufficient incentive to ensure the participation of source countries in drug-discovery programs. The National Cancer Institute or NCI of the U.S. National institutes of Health (NIH), which has been involved in natural product exploration in the third world countries, utilized the legal concept of *quid pro quo* in designing its "Letter of Collection" (LOC). The LOC is a contract that provides for the transfer of technology (and other future benefits), in exchange for access to the biological materials and indigenous knowledge of a source country (Mays et al, 1991). The NCI has used the LOCs to achieve an equitable agreement between a source country for biological materials and research of commercial party. So far, NCI has successfully entered into LOCs with the following countries (or entities within those countries): Bangladesh, Costa Rica, Ecuador, Gabon, Ghana, India, Madagascar, Pakistan, Philippines, Russia, Sarawak, Tanzania, and Zimbabwe.

Plant-derived anticancer drugs identified through the NCI's screening program include the *Vinca* alkaloids (vinblastine and vincristine), etoposide and teniposide, semisynthetic derivatives of epipodophyllotoxin, and taxol (isolated from *Taxus brevifolia* and other species of *Taxus*). Additional anti-cancer drugs are being identified.

NCI-funded contractors have collected plant materials from tropical and subtropical regions of Africa and Madagascar, Central and South America, and Southeast Asia. Additionally, from the Indo-Pacific region, marine organisms, fungi, cyanobacteria, marine anaerobic bacteria, and other protists have been collected.

Inventor in natural-products drug discovery

Under the U.S. Patent Code, the "hero" inventor of the 18th century was replaced by the "team as hero" inventorship, which incorporates a model of collective entrepreneurship (Reich, 1987; Cherensky, 1993). Traditionally, the first to conceive and achieve actual or constructive practice of the claimed invention is recognized as the true inventor. However, in the complex process of natural-product drug discovery many creative persons play key roles. They include indigenous people and traditional healers, botanists, chemists, medical scientists, and clinicians–all playing critical roles in identifying and isolating pharmaceutical agents, leading to eventual drug production for popular use. Under the existing U.S. patent law, the source country and the indigenous people who might provide local knowledge about the medicinal qualities of plants are not generally found to be inventors because such knowledge is not considered novel to the person who possesses it. Traditional knowledge, which is passed on from one generation to the next, does not come under the category of "human ingenuity", a key factor in patent claim approvals. Even under the expanded criteria of U.S patent laws, "team as hero" inventorship model does not recognize the traditional knowledge of indigenous people as "new knowledge" that deserves due recognition.

It is well known that traditional knowledge may play an essential role in the selection of natural biological materials for isolating pharmaceutical agents. For instance, the root of the serpent-wood tree *Rauvolfia serpentina* has been used for centuries in India for the treatment of many diseases including hypertension. after 1967, this became one of the major sources for antihypertensive drugs in the U.S. market (Oldfield, 1989). However, after its transfer to the developed countries, this knowledge becomes intellectual property and is thus patentable. The traditional healer, who supplied the knowledge, is not recognized as a part of the patent ownership.

One solution is a proposed model which incorporates the "chain of invention", but it does not ensure any compensation for the indigenous people who supplied the therapeutic knowledge initially. It has been mentioned by Mays et al (1991) as well as others that the concept of individual ownership of patent rights, based on indigenous knowledge, may be alien to many indigenous societies where property predominantly exists as communal property. However, this should not be a serious obstacle to due recognition for compensation because indigenous societies are certainly aware of, and have no difficulty in accepting, collective rewards or benefits as compensation for their traditional knowledge (e.g. rain dance of the American Indian).

It has been suggested that a new legal concept, that would incorporate non-Western models of intellectual and cultural property, encompassing a broader scope of protection under existing patent law, should be created (Posey, 1994). Others have pointed out that it would be futile to attempt to apply the current patent law to protect traditional knowledge of indigenous communities, because while the underlying policy of the current patent law is to encourage change, the philosophy of indigenous people is to protect and conserve their traditional knowledge (Greaves, 1994). Other suggested models include use of a Contract Law (implying a future benefit) which can be used to full in the gaps in the patent law, a trust or nonprofit corporation that would be similar to the INBio of Costa Rica, or various forms of licensing agreements. The NCI's "Letter of Collection" (LOC) is a contractual agreement that provides for compensation and the transfer of technology to the source country. However, the LOC cannot be used as a mechanism to ensure future intellectual property rights except under CRADA.

NCI's "Letter of Collection" (LOC) addresses a number of issues, including the role and responsibilities of the NCI: conservation and benefits sharing, royalties, technology transfer, patent protection, confidentiality and publication guidelines, licensing, and access to and the use of materials. The source country's responsibilities include: facilitation of collection and export of materials, use of indigenous knowledge to guide collections, provision of raw material and measures for conservation, and use of samples by the host country for other purposes.

The following is a template for NCI's Letter of Collection (LOC). It is an agreement between Source Country and Developmental Therapeutics Program, Division of Cancer Treatment, National Cancer Institute (NCI), National Institutes of Health.

The Developmental Therapeutic Program (DTP), Division of Cancer Treatment (DCT), National Cancer Institute (NCI) is currently investigating plants, marine macro-organisms and microbes as potential sources of novel anticancer and AIDS-antiviral drugs. The DTP is the drug discovery program of the NCI which is an Institute of the National Institutes of Health (NIH), an arm of the Department of Health and Human Services of the United States Government. While investigating the potential of natural products in drug discovery and development, NCI wishes to promote the conservation of biological diversity, and recognizes the need to compensate source country organizations and peoples in the event of commercialization of a drug developed from an organism collected within their borders.

As part of the drug discovery program, DTP has contracts with various organizations for the collection of plants and marine macro-organisms worldwide. DTP has an interest in investigating plants from Source Country, and wishes to collaborate with the Government of Source Country (the Source Country

Governmental) in this investigation. The collection of plants will be within the framework of the collection contract between the NCI and the NCI Contractor, which will collaborate with the Appropriate Agency in Source Country. The NCI will make sincere efforts to transfer knowledge, expertise, and technology related to drug discovery and development to the Appropriate Source Country Institution (SCI) in Source Country as the agent appointed by the Source Country Government, subject to the provision of mutually acceptable guarantees for the protection of intellectual property associated with any patented technology. The Source Country Government, in turn, desires to collaborate closely with the DCT/NCI in pursuit of the investigation of its plats, subject to the conditions and stipulations of this agreement.

The role of DTP, DCT, NCI in the collaboration will include the following.

(1) DTP/NCI will screen the extracts of all plants provided from Source Country for anticancer and AIDS-antiviral activity, and will provide the test results to SCI on a quarterly basis. Such results will be channeled via Contractor.

(2) The test results will be kept confidential by all parties, with any publication delayed until DTP/NCI has an opportunity to file a patent application in the United States of America on any active agents isolated. Such an application will be made according to the terms stated in clause 6.

(3) Any extracts exhibiting significant activity will be further studied by bioassay-guided fractionation in order to isolate the pure compound(s) responsible for the observed activity. Since the relevant bioassays are only available at DTP/NCI, such fractionation will be carried out in DTP/NCI laboratories. A suitably qualified scientist designated by SCI may participate in this process subject to the terms stated in clause 4. In addition, during the course of the contract period, DTP/NCI will assist the Source Country Government, in conjunction with SCI, to develop the capacity to undertake drug discovery and development, including capabilities for the screening and isolation of active compounds from plants and marine organisms.

(4) Subject to the provision that suitable laboratory space and other necessary resources are available, DTP/NCI agree to invite a senior technician or scientist designated by SCI to work in the laboratories using technology which would be useful in furthering work under this agreement. The duration of such a visit would not exceed one year except by prior agreement between SCI and DTP/NCI. The designated Guest Researcher at NIH, except when carrying out research on materials provided through collections in Source Country. Salary and other conditions of exchange will be negotiated in good faith.

(5) In the event of the isolation of a promising agent from a plant collected in Source Country, further development of the agent will be undertaken by DTP/NCI in collaboration with SCI. Once an active agent is approved by the DTP/NCI for preclinical development, SCI and the DTP/NCI will discuss participation by SCI scientists in the development of the specific agent.

The DTP/NCI will make a sincere effort to transfer any knowledge, expertise, and technology developed during such collaboration in the discovery and development process to SCI, subject to the provision of mutually acceptable guarantees for the protection of intellectual property associated with any patented technology.

(6) DTP/NCI will, as appropriate, seek patent protection on all inventions developed under this agreement by DTP/NCI employees alone or by DTP/NCI and Source Country Government employees jointly, and will seek appropriate protection abroad, including in Source Country, if appropriate.

(7) All licenses granted on any patents arising from this collaboration shall contain a clause referring to this agreement and shall indicate that the licensee has been apprised of this agreement.

(8) Should the agent eventually be licensed to a pharmaceutical company for production and marketing, DTP/NCI, will require the successful licensee to negotiate and enter into agreement(s) with the appropriate Source Country Government agency(ies). This agreement(s) will address the concern on the part of the Source Country Government that pertinent agencies, institutions and/or persons receive royalties and other forms of compensation as appropriate.

(9) Such terms shall apply equally to instances where the invention is the actual isolated natural product, or where the invention is a product structurally based on the isolated natural product (i.e. where the natural product provides the lead for development of the invention), though the percentage of royalties negotiated as payment might vary depending upon the relationship of the marketed drug to the originally isolated natural product. It is understood that the eventual development of a drug to the stage of marketing is a long term process which may require 10-15 years.

(10) In obtaining licensees, the DTP/NCI will require the applicant for license to seek as its first source of supply the natural products available from Source Country. If no appropriate licensee is found who will use natural products available from Source Country, or if the Source Country government or its suppliers cannot provide adequate amounts of raw materials at a mutually agreeable fair price, the

licensee will be required to pay to the Source Country Government an amount of money (to be negotiated) to be used for expenses associated with cultivation of medicinal plant species that are endangered by deforestation, or for other appropriate conservation measures. Such terms will also apply to instances where the active agent is prepared by total synthesis.

(11) Section 10 shall not apply to an organism which is freely available from different countries (i.e. common weeds, agricultural crops, ornamental plants, fouling organisms) unless information indicating a particular use of the organism (e.g. medicinal, pesticidal) was provided by local residents to guide the collection of such an organism from Source Country, or unless other justification acceptable to both the Source Country Government and DTP/NCI is provided. In the case where an organism is freely available from different countries, but a genotype producing an active agent is found only in source Country, section 10 shall apply.

(12) DTP/NCI will test any pure compounds submitted by Source Country Government and SCI scientists for antitumor and AIDS-antiviral activity, provided such compounds have not been tested previously in the DTP/NCI screens. If significant antitumor or AIDS-antiviral activity is detected, further development of the compound and investigation of patent rights will, as appropriate, be undertaken by DTP/NCI in consultation with SCI and the Source Country Government.

Should the agent eventually be licensed to a pharmaceutical company for production and marketing, DTP/NCI will require the successful licensee to negotiate and enter into agreement(s) with the appropriate Source Country Government agency(ies). This agreement will address the concern on the part of the source country Government that pertinent agencies, institutions and/or persons receive royalties and other forms of compensation, as appropriate.

(13) DTP/NCI may send selected samples to other organizations for investigation of their anticancer, anti-HIV or other therapeutic potential. Such samples will be restricted to those collected by NCI contractors, unless specifically authorized by the Source Country Government. Any organization receiving samples must agree to compensate the Source Country Government and individuals, as appropriate, in the same fashion as is described in sections 8-10 above, notwithstanding anything the country in section 11.

The role of the Source Country Government in the collaboration will include the following:

(1) The Appropriate Agency in Source Country will collaborate with Contractor in the collection of plants, and will work with Contractor to arrange the necessary permits to ensure the timely collection and export of materials to DTP/NCI.

(2) Should the Appropriate Agency in Source Country have any knowledge of the medicinal use of any plants by the local population or traditionally healers, this information will be used to guide the collection of plants on a priority basis where possible. Detail of the methods of administration (e.g. hot infusion, etc.) used by the traditional healers will be provided where applicable to enable suitable extracts to be made. All such information will be held confidential by DTP/NCI until both parties agree to publication.

The permission of the traditional healer or community will be sought before publication of their information, and proper acknowledgment will be made of their contribution.

(3) The Appropriate Agency in Source Country and Contractor will collaborate in the provision of further quantities of active raw material if required for development studies.

(4) In the event of large amounts of raw material being required for production, the Appropriate Agency in Source Country and Contractor will investigate the mass propagation of the material in Source Country. Consideration should also be given to sustainable harvest of the material while conserving the biological diversity of the region, and involvement of the local population in the planning and implementation stages.

(5) Source Country Government and SCI scientists and their collaborators may screen additional samples of the same raw materials for other biological activities and develop them for such purposes independently of this agreement.

This agreement may be amended at any time subject to the written agreement of both parties.

Name (Print or Type)
Institution or Agency
Address
Date

Director
National Cancer Institute
Date:

Table 9.5 Number of threatened species

Species	Endangered	Vulnerable	Total
Mammals	177	199	376
Birds	188	241	49
Reptiles	47	88	135
Amphibians	32	32	64
Fishes	158	226	384
Invertebrates	582	702	1284
Plants	3632	5687	9319
Total	4816	7175	11991

Source: The World Conservation Monitoring Center, 1995

10 Patenting cDNA sequences: the NIH controversy

It is of interest to discuss briefly the international patent, filed by the Secretary, Department of Health & Human Services, U.S. Government, on behalf of the inventors, Craig J. Ventor and Mark D. Adams, on 19 June, 1992. The title of the patent is: "Sequences characteristic of human gene transcription product".

Abstract

Partial and complete human cDNA and genomic sequences correspond to particular expressed sequence tags (ESTs). The ESTs are cDNA sequences that (a) are generally between 150 and 500 base pairs in length, (b) are derived from human brain cDNA libraries, (c) correspond to genes transcribed in human brain, and (d) have base sequences identified herein as SEQ ID NOS: 1-315.

The invention relates to newly identified polynucleotide sequences corresponding to transcription products of human genes, and to the complete gene sequences associated with them.

Although later the NIH, under its new leadership, decided not to pursue these patent rights, the controversy provides a unique example for considering the issues involved in gene patenting in the context of technology transfer (Anderson, 1994).

The patent application filed by Ventor and Adams was a sweeping one, broadly encompassing cDNA sequencing of the human genome. Quite understandably, others who have been working in the same field have challenged their claim. Ventor and Adams have stated that:

> Contrary to the expectations of the scientific community, cDNA screening and sequencing techniques have now been used to discover a large number of heretofore unknown human genes. Disclosed herein are over 300 new human polynucleotide sequences. The novelty of these sequences has been established through comparison to both nucleotide sequence databases and amino acid sequence databases.

Surprisingly, approximately 80% of the sequences generated were unrelated to any sequences previously described in the literature.

The rationale for the filing is that patent protection may be necessary to ensure that private firms are willing to invest in developing related products, because (a) NIH may obtain patent rights that will offer effective product monopolies to licensee firms, and (b) that unless NIH obtains these rights now, firms will be unable to obtain a comparable degree of exclusivity by other means, such as by obtaining patents of their own subsequent innovations (Eisenberg, 1992). There is good reason to doubt that these justifications are valid. Opponents have argued that the issuance of patents to those who randomly sequence partial cDNAs could discourage firms to undertake the more costly work of systematic gene mapping. On the other hand, the NIH Director claimed that patent protection was necessary to ensure that private companies would be willing to develop gene-related products.

What is patentable?

The NIH application contained claims not only to the partial cDNA sequences as isolated molecules but also to longer sequences that incorporate the partial cDNAs. However, some major objections may be cited. First, intuitively one can argue that patents should not be issued for the discovery of things which already exist in nature. A 1948 decision by the Supreme court rejected a patent claim to a mixed culture of naturally occurring bacteria because "The qualities of these bacteria, like the heat of the sun, electricity, or the qualities of metals, are part of the storehouse of knowledge of all men. They are manifestations of laws of nature, free to all men and reserved exclusively to none". On the other hand, in the case of *Diamond vs. Chakrabarty*, the Supreme Court ruled that "anything under the sun that is made by man" is patentable. It can be easily argued that cDNA sequences are manifestations of laws of nature. However, lower courts have upheld patents on purified chemicals and biologically pure cultures of naturally occurring micro-organisms (see Eisenberg, 1992 for details). A second ground for rejection is when the utility of the patent is unknown. That was indeed the case with respect to the cDNA partial sequences of the NIH patent. The relevant genes, or the proteins those genes code for, or the functions those proteins perform were not identified. In *Brenner vs. Manson*, the Supreme Court ruled that a claim to a process of making a novel steroid was invalid because it was not shown to have any practical application (1966). NIH had anticipated this objection by stating that the cDNA sequences may be used as genetic markers, for forensic identification, or for tissue typing.

NIH's claim that its patenting of cDNA sequences would stimulate greater investment by the private industry in developing the gene products was contradicted by the Pharmaceutical Manufacturers Association (PMA) as well as two biotechnology trade groups that have since merged (the Industrial Biotechnology Association or IBA, and the Association of Biotechnology Companies or ABC). Both the PMA and IBA urged NIH not to seek patent protection on DNA sequences with no known biological function. They argued that such sequences should be freely available to the public. On the other hand, ABC agreed with the NIH's decision to seek patent protection but urged that the patents be licensed on a nonexclusive basis so that industrial development projects can proceed freely without hindrance. It was implied that exclusive rights in discoveries could interfere with the commercial product development.

Eisenberg (1994) stated that:

> the course of scientific discovery and product development is incredibly complex and variable and unpredictable. Neither the old-fashioned approach of leaving all new discoveries in the public domain, nor the current approach of assigning exclusive rights in such discoveries to private parties, should be uniformly applied across the entire range of publicly supported discoveries.

The U.S. Government's policy in technology transfer has been defined by two Congressional statutes passed in 1980; (a) the Stevenson-Wydler Technology Innovation Act, which made technology transfer an integral part of the R & D responsibilities of federal laboratories and their employees; and (b) the Bayh-Dole Act, which dealt specifically with the role of patents in technology transfer. The latter reversed the then existing practice of some federal agencies retaining public ownership of inventions made outside the government with federal funds. It provided an incentive for small businesses and nonprofit organizations to promote commercial development of inventions and retain patent ownership themselves. In 1984, the U.S. Congress passed a series of amendments which extended these incentives to both government-owned as well as contractor-operated facilities, and finally, in 1986, the Congress authorized federal laboratories to enter into cooperative research and development agreements, including patent rights, with both the public and private sectors (see Eisenberg, 1994).

Do patents promote technology transfer?

Whether a patent proves to be an incentive or a hindrance to subsequent research and development depends very much on the nature of the patent itself. A patent is at its best when it covers an end product which can be sold to customers. On the other hand, a patent on a research device or technique that is required for subsequent development may complicate the process of providing an incentive and slow down progress. At its best, a patent is meant to provide an incentive to develop products, enjoy the benefits of their investment, and eliminate competition out of their markets, at least temporarily.

The cDNA patent discussed above belongs to the latter category because it is concerned with an intermediate step that may possibly lead to unspecified product development subsequently. Among the many controversies that surrounded the cDNA patent issue are the following. It created a general mistrust in the scientific community that a few pioneers, who happened to be ahead of others, were trying to appropriate the intellectual property rights to a far greater extent than their realistic achievements. It was an attempt on their part to lay claim to future discoveries and applications in that arena. It raised the question of fairness and efficacy of the entire system which was instituted in the first place to ensure an equitable distribution of rewards in proportion to incentives and achievements.

Free access to knowledge or investment in R & D?

The fact of the matter is that until recently most scientists have given little thought to the commercial application of their discoveries. Contrary to the prevailing custom, their cause was championed by a public institution, the NIH, not the private research industry. Following the NIH lead, the major pharmaceutical firm of Merck & Co. eventually sponsored a university-based effort to place such information in the public sector. Eisenberg (1996) has admirably discussed the pros and cons of this debate. This discussion is taking an increasingly important place not only among the scientists but also in the general population which is becoming increasingly aware of the potential impact of the human genomic research. The NIH controversy has been useful in drawing attention to a number of vital issues which were not adequately addressed in previous years.

The basic question underlying the controversy is this: where do we draw the line between access to knowledge on the one hand and the need to create incentives for increased investments in research and development on the other? There are at least three reasons for following the path of patenting; (a) one is to protect the copyright or intellectual property from unauthorized usage, (b) the second reason is to earn monetary rewards from selling that copyright to others, and (c) the third is to provide an incentive by setting an example of the kind of rewards one may expect by following the path of patenting, which in turn will stimulate further research and development by other. Protection from competition will encourage post-invention development.

In this manner, patents will encourage transfer of technology from the public sector to the private sector.

Eisenberg (1996) and others have argued that the patenting of cDNA sequences by Venter and his colleagues may be the kind of research discovery that is best left in the public sector. As was evident later, the NIH patent claim was subsequently rejected by the U.S Patent and Trademark Office (PTO) and those particular sequences entered the public domain (Anderson, 1994). Consequently, in 1992, Venter and his collaborators left the NIH, and founded the non-profit research organization, The Institute for Genomic Research, in Rockville, Maryland, with the generous backing of private-sector funds. A separate, for-profit company, Human Genome Sciences, was also established (by the same financial backers) to develop commercial products from the database established by its sister organization, The Institute for Genomic Research. Other databases are also being established simultaneously both in the U.S. (Incyte Pharmaceuticals, Palo Alto, CA) and also abroad, especially in France and England.

Patenting DNA fragments, a mistake?

A number of prominent scientists including J.D. Watson have opposed the patenting of DNA fragments which the NIH Director Bernadine Healy had supported a few years ago. Indeed, Watson had resigned in protest from his position as Associate Director in-charge of the Human Genome Project at the National Institutes of Health. Some others who are not scientists have also expressed reservations about the patenting of DNA sequences (under the direction of Craig Venter). An attorney who specialized in biotechnology, Thomas D. Kiley, commented:

The proposal by the National Institutes of Health (NIH) to patent products resulting merely from sequencing the human genome is a mistake: at worse, it is wrong in patent law; at best, it relies on deficiency in law concerning what is "useful" as a requirement for patents. The proposal is symptomatic of a problem besieging biotechnology–attempts to control the raw material of scientific experimentation before research has determined the practical value of such material–that needs curing on many fronts.

In his paper in *Science*, Kiley (1992) proposed corrective measures which should be adopted by the Executive Branch, the Congress, and the Courts in the United States.

Kiley stated that the trend in biotechnology law is debilitating the growth of science. Since the patent statute clearly requires that, to be patentable, inventions must first be shown to be "useful", there are reasonable grounds to object to patenting sequences with no known utility. Kiley (1992) had commented that the NIH proposal is symptomatic of an increasingly widespread practice in biotechnology that is attempting to control not discoveries but the means to make discoveries. Judicial and legislative remedies may be needed to restore order to the onslaught of patents that are being fashioned to control not the finished product but the basic raw materials. It is also true that government policy in the 1980s has changed to provide grants that may lead to patentable inventions even though they are funded by public funds. In other words, government funds research but it is private investors who support the work leading to the transformation of those research results into inventions ready for consumption by the public.

Even though the NIH patents of DNA sequences are only of historic interest at present they do raise an important question of basic policy which may come up again in the future with respect to research in other areas. There is another twist to the patenting of DNA sequences but not their product. Overseas manufacturers may be able to export the unpatented protein to the United States.

There is abundant evidence to indicate that the U.S. Supreme Court would rule in opposition to the patenting of incomplete processes with no clearly defined use to the public. Kiley (1992) cited the case of Brenner v. Manson when the Court rejected claims to 2-methyldihydroxytestosterone derivatives, whose sole utility "consist in (their) potential role as an object of use-testing" (in the words of the Court). The Court stated that such claims "may confer power to block off whole areas of scientific development without compensating benefit to the public. . . . A patent is not a hunting license. It is not a reward for the search, but compensation for its successful conclusion". The Court further stated that since a patent system must be related to the world of commerce rather than to the realm of philosophy, what is needed is "substantial" utility representing "specific benefit in currently available form". Kiley (1992) commented that the utilities concocted by the NIH to carry the patents (such as for use in chromosome mapping or in distinguishing brain-specific transcripts from others) are merely excuses until someone finds out what the DNA is really good for. Kiley (1992) wrote further: "Since the real purpose of the application is to control individual DNAs and thereby commerce in the proteins they encode, this approach, in my opinion, amounts to a cynical resort to deficiencies in the law concerning what utility is sufficient for patents".

Benefit to the public

In this entire discussion, I have considered the NIH patents for DNA sequences because, though unsuccessful, they indicate an increasing trend in biotechnology to file patents of obscure utility. It has been suggested that sole reliance on the Supreme Court may not serve the best interests of either commerce or science in this matter, but the congress may be better situated to resolve the complex issues involved. As Kiley (1992) noted:

> Congress should change law that now permits research efforts that use patented inventions to be shut down. The object would be to free scientific research wherever it gets done from the threat of foreclosure by injunction. The new criterion for injunction should be whether an already patented invention is itself placed into the stream of commerce, as distinct from its being used en route to the invention of a different thing. The middle ground, where research for hire uses someone else's patented invention, should be immunized from judicial foreclosure in the interest of encouraging new discoveries.

It has been suggested further that it would be useful to amend the patent statute to provide explicitly for product patents on "old" substances when new uses have been found for them. This practice is followed in Europe. This would eliminate the kind of justification which the NIH had claimed in the past that patent claims are required to prevent publication because it may remove incentive to develop. Under these new rules, the patent would be won by those who successfully invent products of practical utility not mere catalogue of DNA sequences.

The case for genomic patenting

The case for genomic patenting has been strongly advocated by George Poste (1995), whose position is clearly understandable when we realize that he is associated with SmithKline Beecham Pharmaceuticals. It is of interest to examine this position carefully because it is obviously relevant to the whole question of intellectual property rights and technology transfer. Poste begins by stating that the borders between academic research and industrial research are increasingly blurred in recent years. Many academics have helped to establish new companies in which they (and their academic institutions) hold financial interests. They have benefited from intellectual property rights related to their inventions which have been, in fact, financed by taxpayer-sponsored government funds. Therein lies an ethical problem—public funds for private profit-making ventures? Poste wrote: "Here I present the case for genomic patents, challenge the claim that they impede research and examine the implications of proposals that human gene sequences should not be patented but placed in the public domain"

Three different kinds of concerns may be discerned, each representing a particular lobby: (a) the academic and research communities are primarily concerned about whether the patenting process would destroy the free and open exchange of information that has been the hallmark of excellence in research, (b) on the other side, there are also anti-science anti-technology protest lobbies (for instance, the Foundation for Economic Trends founded by Jeremy Rifkin) who are joining forces with various religious groups, expressing their concerns on moral and ethical grounds, and (c) finally, the industrial lobby which is mainly concerned with the commercial possibilities of genetic technology.

Principles of patenting

There are three major criteria which need to be fulfilled to satisfy the patenting regulations : (a) novelty (not previously known), (b) nonobviousness (invented by human ingenuity), and (c) utility (practical application). There is a widespread belief that patenting genes does not meet the criteria required. A gene may not be known previously, but the process of making it known can be regarded as a discovery, not an invention. The question that is asked frequently is: "How can you invent something that already exists in nature?" Poste answered as follows: "The skills required to construct full-length genes and define their function and utility are not straightforward. . . . They have been accepted by patent authorities in Europe, the United States and Japan as evidence of inventiveness, with rapid growth in the number of gene patents awarded". To some, this response may seem inadequate because a discovery may be brought on by inventive techniques but the basic finding still remains a discovery, not an invention. We shall return to this question later on.

The second major objection is that the mere process of knowing a sequence of genes does not reveal its utility. Before we can exploit this knowledge for commercial purposes, further research–both basic and applied–will be required. For that reason, many see the patent claims for DNA sequences as too premature. This was the situation in 1992 when the National Institutes of Health (NIH) decided to seek 'omnibus' patents for several thousand complementary DNA fragments, or expression-sequence tags (ESTs), with no known function. Faced with widespread opposition, the NIH withdrew its patent claim. But the incident was useful in raising a number of legal and ethical issues related to biotechnology and intellectual property rights.

With respect to the patenting of ESTs, Poste (1995) stated that they should be patentable if their novelty, inventiveness and utility can be demonstrated, but their utility can be demonstrated. However, their utility may be limited to a role in diagnostic fingerprinting for disease detection or staging. In principle, HUGO (Human Genome Organization) has expressed support for genomic patents if the three major criteria are satisfied. However, some concern remains among various parties contributing to the research effort. There is also concern regarding the conflicting interests of basic research as opposed to product development. One method of resolving the question of equity is to negotiate co-inventorship which was suggested by the NIH for the *BRCA-1* claim, adding its own scientists as co-inventors to those of Myriad Genetics.

European patent laws contain specific provisions to reject claims on the grounds of moral offensiveness or threat to public order. However, the morality question is applied to the exploitation of the invention, not the invention itself. Morality itself is a changing concept which does not provide us with lasting answers. What is considered 'moral' today may not be so in the future and vice versa.

U.K. parliamentary report

Contrary to the U.S. position, the British House of Commons has clearly opposed the patenting of DNA sequences. An all-party committee of Britain's House of Commons stated that patenting should not be allowed on "naturally occurring nucleotide sequences" because it is considered as "pure knowledge"–and thus should not be patented (Dickson, 1995). Their position is best expressed by one committee member: "Our concern is that if someone discovers and then patents a particular gene, that will increasingly complicate, slow down and make more expensive the process of working out its interaction with other genes in the human body". Later, the U.K. parliamentary report on human genetics expressed concern that "patent examiners are applying the criteria of utility and novelty too loosely". They have urged the European Patent Convention to reconsider the patent regulations to make them more rigorous when applied to basic research in human genetics. The European Union insisted on a strong ethical framework and worked out a compromise formula. However, the Green Party continues to express strong opposition to the patenting of human genes and transgenic animals. To those who argue that patenting of genes impedes the progress of basic research, Poste (1995) responded as follows:

> Yet academic institutions now rank with industry in the intense pursuit of patents on molecules used by the basic research community . . . . patent law already provides a broad exemption for the use of proprietary materials for 'research purposes' . . . A ban on patenting genomic inventions would invariably mean that companies, or any party, wishing to use the knowledge to create products would resort to trade secrecy. This would slow research, with inventors, academic and industrial, withholding knowledge to the detriment of the overall research community.

Poste argued that "secrecy would create a destructive, anti-intellectual climate at a time when ties between academic institutions and industry in the life science are prospering. . . . Those seeking to pioneer genetic medicine might usefully reflect on the fate of the nuclear power industry and the consequences of failure to educate and inform a concerned public". As discussed elsewhere, while SmithKline Beecham's policy is much more patent-oriented, Merck funded the public database of human cDNAs at Washington University in St. Louis with the specific goal of accelerating the gene discovery process and to benefit human health. Merck regarded that the discovery of genes and proteins would only rarely be of direct therapeutic value, if any. Its main value lies in its use as a research tool. On the other hand, the position of SmithKline Beecham, as stated by Poste (1995), is that the patenting of human genes is needed to protect intellectual property rights and thus provide an incentive for the research and development of new drug and diagnostics.

At a conference organized by the French Academy of Sciences in Paris in 1995, genetic scientists varied considerably in their attitude towards gene patenting (Butler, 1995). The Director General of INSERM, the French biomedical research organization, Philippe Lazar, said: "Patenting genes poses no specific problems . . . Patents are the instruments of partnership between science and the economy". On the other hand, some scientists such as Jean Weissenback of the French Genome Center, Genethon, argued that finding a gene is not inventive. Some others stated that it is not unusual for patent offices to grant broad patents in the early days of a new technology, and to narrow the focus as the technology unfolds. Some lawyers at the conference commented that the scientists' concern that patents would stifle further research is unwarranted because separate patent rights are now conferred on new applications of existing drug molecules. Others at the conference believed that most of the present doubts about the desirability of patenting would disappear over time. The key problem for the future would be the enforcement of patent rights.

Public and private databases

An alternative to patent protection is to protect databases by controlling access to them by means of contracts and by following trade secrecy policies. However, as the information in the public domain increases the value of private databases diminishes rapidly. This was indeed the case with Merck's sponsorship of a competing cDNA-sequencing program at Washington University in St. Louis. Although the public databases are growing rapidly, the private databases are significantly larger at present. However, owners of private databases are making claims which seem to make their product appear to be superior in quality. These claims include the availability of contiguous fragments of cDNA into longer sequences, more complete annotations for the sequences, and the availability of high-powered bioinformatics capabilities and user-friendly software. However, as sequences in the public database are being mapped and the mapping information is being made readily available to the public, their value is enhanced, especially for positional cloning (see Boguski and Schuler, Nat Genet, 10, 369-371, 1995; Collins, Nat Genet, 9, 347-350, 1995).

However, there are certain complications. If patents are issued to private database owners, they could pre-empt the use of any sequences covered by them, even those that are publicly disclosed before the patents are issued, as long as they are able to establish their priority. This situation is further complicated because the secrecy that surrounds U.S. patent applications makes it impossible to foresee which sequences might be covered, and one can never be sure how long those sequences will remain in the public domain. Of course, the same fate awaits sequences from the private databases as well because they may be already covered by a previously filed patent by another group.

SmithKline Beecham (SB) paid $125 milion (plus royalties on product sales) for a three-year exclusive right of access to the database of Human Genomic Sciences (HGS), a for-profit company mentioned earlier. SB acquired the "right of first refusal" to develop and market therapeutic and diagnostic products which may result from using this database. However, the agreement does not include gene therapy or anti-sense products. HGS has signed separate agreements with other institutions in these areas. In addition, academic and non-profit institutions may enter into limited agreements with HGS to obtain access to certain portions of the database. And academic non-profit investigators may access sequences which have already been disclosed or partially disclosed on less- restricted terms, but the door is totally closed to commercial investigators. Recently, HGS and SB have collaborated to allow four pharmaceutical firms to share access to the database and initiate product development. These companies are Takeda Chemical, Merck KG&A, Schering Plough, Synthelabo SA. In addition to providing additional funds to HGS and SB, these agreements will expand greatly the number of participating investigators and create new opportunities for research and development.

As opposed to exclusive licensing, Pharmacia & Upjohn and Pfizer have signed separate non-exclusive agreements with Incyte, and later several other pharmaceutical firms including Johnson & Johnson, Hoffman-La Roche and Abbott Laboratories have also signed similar agreements with Incyte.

Merck's strategy

Merck's strategy of making a small investment to place sequence information in the public domain is seen by some as a plan to undermine the value of investments already made by its commercial competitors. Such a strategy would force Incyte,

HGS and their collaborators to seek patent rights to protect their investments. Merck may be betting that those patent rights will be scarce. On the other hand, Merck may be waiting until the sequence information is developed further to a stage when commercial development becomes a reality. Its resources then will be able to cash in on the product development.

The position taken by Merck is of interest from the viewpoint of the relative roles of public and private initiatives in stimulating research and development. The boundaries between private and public investments in research and development are blurred in this case. Eisenberg (1996) pointed out that in such fields with commercial interest as genomics, scientists in both public and private groups are concerned with similar problems. Some believe that those who are involved in publicly sponsored research should promote commercial development by patenting their discoveries. There is some agreement that free access to information encourages to wider applications because it minimizes cost as well as procedural delays which would slow down the pace of development because of the need to negotiate licenses for access to private information and previous discoveries. A vigorous public sector would also enhance contacts between diverse individuals and groups, leading to a vigorous debate that would create a far healthier climate for research and development. Merck obviously believes in this project as its investment in the public domain at Washington University clearly indicates. This particular instance has reinforced the value of maintaining a healthy public sector to promote research and development. However, it is also clear that we cannot entirely depend on the private sector to enrich the public domain when public research institutions are pursuing patent development in competition with the private sector.

Genomic sequence information in the public domain

David Bentley (1996), of the Sanger Center in Cambridge, U.K., presented arguments in favor of immediately releasing sequence information. He wrote:

> The finished sequence should be released directly upon completion. Furthermore, there should be an earlier prerelease of unfinished sequence and additional mapping information. This is required to optimize coordination, independent checking, and exploitation in both academic and commercial laboratories.

To minimize the risk of costly duplication it is necessary to provide regularly updated maps of all clones as soon as they enter the process. Progress is then monitored by the prerelease of the unfinished sequence of each clone. Informal prerelease provides most of the sequence information to the public promptly. Citing the example of the determination of the structure of the BRCA2 and its association with familial breast cancer, Bentley (1996) argued that unfinished sequence data contain information which is sufficient for many biological and genetic studies. He advocates maximum accessibility of the human genome sequence for "interpretation and exploitation", both in the academic as well as the commercial sectors.

On the other hand, Adams and Venter (1996) cautioned about using or releasing data that had not been extensively peer-reviewed or self-reviewed. They expressed concern that raw or finished sequence data release without accompanying scientific publications may become the norm for contributions by some groups. They suggested further that scientific journals should develop policies

> that either deal with prepublication release of data or make it clear to the community that current policies will remain in effect. Will peer reviewers in the future decide that the novelty of a manuscript has been compromised if the annotated sequence is fully available on the Internet?

Another problem is utility of a DNA sequence information by itself. Surely, it is necessary to answer other questions such as how to define genes, regulatory sites, and repetitive data and also how the final structure was determined. Adams and Venter (1996) speculated that if the human genome is to be completely sequenced over the next 7 to 10 years it would require the finishing and publication of about 500 million base pairs of sequence each year, that is to say "the equivalent of the *E. coli* genome being published every 2 days for the next 7 years"–and that is only the human genome project, and does not include the sequencing of the genomes of several other species which is under way by several groups. It would be hard to maintain the highest standards of data collection, analysis, scientific interpretation, completion and publication of the daily released data which will be emanating from this enormous project. Adams and Venter (1996) have argued in favor of publishing complete scientific papers within a reasonable interval. Such publications should include methods of data collection and analysis as well as the scientific significance within a broader biological context.

11 NIH patent policy

The United States Public Health Service Technology Transfer Manual has been recently revised and updated. In 1986, U.S. Federal laboratories, including the laboratories of the National Institutes of Health (NIH), Food and Drug Administration (FDA), and Centers for Disease Control and Prevention (CDC), were given a mandate to facilitate the transfer of new technologies, developed in those laboratories, to the private sector for commercialization in an expeditious manner. Obviously, adequate patent protection in the United States and abroad is a strong incentive for the private sector initiative. Some ground rules regarding the PHS policy for patenting are as follows:

(1) The PHS will seek patent protection on biomedical technologies only when the patent facilitates availability of the technology to the public for preventive, diagnostic, therapeutic, or research use, or other commercial use.

(2) Patent protection will not be sought by the PHS where further research and development is not necessary to realize the technology's primary use and anticipated future applications.

(3) PHS will not seek patent protection on a technology unless its commercial or public health value warrants the expenditure of funds for patenting.

(4) Patent protection will not be sought also in cases where commercialization and technology transfer can be accomplished without the need to apply for patent protection.

(5) When the results are obtained under a Cooperative Research and Development Agreement (CRADA), an evaluation will be made whether a patent can be filed in accordance with the terms of the CRADA.

(6) The process of filing patent applications will not be allowed to delay the publication of research results.

(7) When research is in the early stages of development, a patent will be filed only on research that has a practical utility or a reasonable expectation of future practical utility. For example, "the practical utility of a cDNA sequence is determined according to whether a potential use is directly a consequence of the particular sequence, not a use common to all DNA".

(8) Once a patent is initiated, maintenance of patent applications and issued patents will continue only as long as there remains a reasonable expectation of transferring the patent rights to a commercial partner through licensing.

(9) Any litigation to enforce and defend patents in the Federal Court system will be pursued only with the approval of the Justice Department.

PHS licensing policy

The U.S. Public Health Service outlined its policy for licensing technologies developed in PHS laboratories which have been listed earlier. It is necessary for a patent to attract investment by commercial partners to promote further research and commercial development of the technology. This is critical when there is potential for developing preventive, diagnostic, or therapeutic products. However, in some instances, technologies may be transferred to the private sector expeditionary through publication.

Each technology is developed for the broadest possible applications. First, the inventorship (and thus ownership) rights to PHS technologies is diligently ascertained in accordance with the patent law. Second, PHS retains the ownership rights for transfer to the private sector through licensing instead of assignment. This policy allows the PHS to promote through licensing negotiations.

More than one company may develop products from a particular technology by negotiating non-exclusive or co-exclusive licenses whenever possible. A company may frequently add its own proprietary technologies to the technology licensed from the government to ultimately achieve some level of uniqueness and exclusively for the final product.

Although a technology may be licensed for commercial development, PHS continues to make that technology available for further research by non-profit and for-profit entities. Furthermore, PHS requires that exclusive licenses grant sublicenses to broaden the development of products when necessary for the public health. This situation particularly applies to CRADA exclusive licenses which are granted to patents arising under the CRADA, and are generally broad in their scope for research and development.

PHS encourages expeditious commercial development by (a) granting license rights only to develop certain fields for which the company is most suited, by (b) monitoring the pace of development by negotiating commercial development milestones with proposed licensees, and by (c) negotiating license execution fees, minimum annual royalty payments, and reimbursement of patent expenses in addition to earned royalty payments.

PHS promotes public access to the benefits of its technology by fostering the development of competing products for same or similar applications. PHS negotiates and obtains public benefits from licensees that are consistent with expeditious commercial development and accessibility of the technology. PHS reserves the right to fully develop the rights granted.

Notice of availability of inventions for licensing

There are different kinds of licensing for U.S. Government-owned inventions. The following are some examples.

(a) General promotion
Reducing cytopathicityin T cells infected by lentivirus:

> The patent involves a new process capable of limiting T-cell death (T-cell syncytium formation) initiated by HIV-1 infection has been discovered. It is believed that such cell death may be due to intracellular signals transmitted when HIV-1 envelope gycoproteins interact with their cellular receptor, CD4, and other receptors on a second cell. When certain intracellular signals associated with HIV-1 envelope are blocked, the cellular changes triggered by HIV also are dramatically inhibited. These experiments employed a new T-cell line (HIVenv2-8) stably transfected to express all of the HIV envelope glycoproteins, including gp160, and gp120, and gp41. This cell line has been used to find that a specific inhibitor of protein tyrosine kinases, herbimycin A, reduced HIV envelope-associated syncytium formation and thus may be a basis for treatment of HIV infection.

(b) Special promotion
U.S. Patent 4,405,712, issued on September 20, 1983 and entitled "LTR-Vectors": This is a broad patent which claims processes of obtaining the expression of any gene via the use of retroviral expression vectors containing long terminal repear (LTR) sequences. The invention is of fundamental significance for the retroviral mediated expression of genes *in vitro* for research and biopharmaceutical production and *in vivo* for research, biopharmaceutical production and therapeutic applications, such as somatic cell gene therapy. This invention was licensed on a non-exclusive basis.

(c) Exclusive license

The invention is a novel surgical implantation method, which involves implantation into the brain of suitable histocompatible leukocytes activated by lymphkines, cytokines, etc. It involves an improved method of treating Parkinson's disease and other diseases that affect the dopaminergic system. It can reduce or eliminate L-Dope therapy, which has significant toxic side effects. Patient's own autologous leukocytes are used, thus reducing the chance of host rejection.

All patents are generally made available for licensing in the U.S., to achieve expeditious commercialization of results of federally funded research and development. Foreign patent applications are filed on selected inventions.

Table 11.1 NIH foreign filing procedure for U.S. filed patent applications

Timeline (weeks before filing deadline)	Individual response	Action
20 weeks	Foreign Filing Coordinator (FFC)	Develops assignment schedule/requirements
20 weeks	Licensing Specialist	Receives case assignment, Conducts and coordinates licensing review and evaluates patent status
16 weeks	Licensing Specialist	Provides draft recommendation to Lead Licensing Specialist of Working Group
13 weeks	Licensing Specialist	Submits checklist and final memorandum to FFC

Table 11.1 NIH foreign filing procedure for U.S. filed patent applications (continued)

Timeline (weeks before filing deadline)	Individual response	Action
12 weeks	Foreign Filing Coordinator	Sends memorandum to Technology Development Coordinators (TDC)
8 weeks	Foreign Filing Coordinator	Ensures that response is received from TDC. If consistent with Office of Technology Transfer (OTT) recommendation, issues work order to contracting firm, ensures that copy of work order and TDC response is personally delivered to patent advisor
7 weeks	Patent Advisor	Reviews foreign filing work order report and ensures that firm has faxed back estimate. The estimate is entered into records, signed and returned to firm in enough time to allow completion of work by filing deadline.

PHS Cooperative Research and Development Agreement Policy

The following is a policy outline for conducting Cooperative Research and Development Agreements (CRADAs) within U.S. Public Health Service (PHS) laboratories including the National Institutes of Health. Under the Federal Technology Transfer ACT (FTTA) of 1986, and Executive Order No. 12591, the Public Health Service has been mandated to encourage and facilitate collaboration among federal laboratories, state and local governments, universities, and the private sector in order to assist in the transfer of federal technology to the market place. CRADA provides a mechanism to facilitate this collaboration. It is an agreement between one or more PHS laboratories and one or more non-federal parties. Under such an agreements, the PHS laboratories provide personnel, services, facilities, equipment, or other resources toward the conduct of specified research or development efforts. However, the federal laboratories do not provide funds to non-federal parties. CRADAs do not confer intellectual property rights in PHS inventions to non-federal parties.

CRADAs were established by the U.S. Congress to promote technological competitiveness and the rapid transfer of the new inventions for commercial exploitation. By this process, new knowledge is transferred rapidly to various non-federal agencies and other groups, private sector and the universities. Underlying this policy is the realization that a free flow of information and discourse is essential for a healthy economy and for further research and development. All CRADA research projects must be highly focused and delineated with a clear and specific objective. The proposed collaborator's research and business capabilities will be carefully evaluated.

This mechanism is not meant to be a source of funds for research and should not be a major source of support for either the PHS laboratory or its non-federal collaborator. PHS investigators are generally free to choose the subject matter of their research that is consistent with the overall objectives of their institutes and laboratories. Although public discussion of results is encouraged, reasonable confidentiality and delay in dissemination are occasionally allowed under a CRADA, to protect propriety materials and intellectual property rights. Outside organizations are encouraged to establish meaningful collaborations under a CRADA. However, routine or conventional testing, with no intellectual contribution from the collaborator, are considered inappropriate. Although PHS policy promotes fair access to collaboration with a PHS laboratory under a CRADA, it is not to be considered as an "open competition" (*Technology Transfer Policy Manual*, NIH Office of Technology Transfer, 1996).

Other aspects of agreements

Recipients are cautioned to exercise great sensitivity in the development of sponsored research agreements. Care is taken to make sure that a sponsored research agreement does not adversely affect PHS funded programs and recipient concerns such as academic freedom, or scientific activities and management.

Four points are of special concern:

(1) Heightened scrutiny is required under the following conditions:
   (a) financial support from the sponsor is at least $ 5 million or higher in any one year, or $ 50 million total over the total funding period;
   (b) the proportion of funding by the sponsor is over 20 per cent of the recipient's total research funding;
   (c) the sponsor's prospective licensing rights cover all technologies developed by a major constituent of the recipient organization (such as a department), or the technologies involved represent a substantial proportion of the potential intellectual contribution of the recipient organization; or
   (d) the duration of the proposed agreement exceeds five years.

It is believed that, if one or more of these criteria apply, it is likely that the proposed agreement will adversely impact on the likelihood of commercial access, particularly for small business. Under such circumstances, rapid development and commercialization of technology would be delayed.

(2) If the sponsored agreement is too broad, covering a wide array of recipient research findings and technologies, it would effectively exclude any access to recipient's technology by other organizations. It would then eliminate competition and impede rapid commercialization of technology.

(3) If the sponsor provides funds for general operations rather than specific research projects, that funding should be considered in relation to funds from other sources when the question of sharing intellectual property rights is considered. Both the level of funding as well as the degree of risk assumed (by the sponsor) should be taken to account when intellectual property rights are considered. The sponsor's rights may be limited to a certain segment or percentage of the inventions for set period of time.

(4) Recipient should not enter into any unusual agreements or practices that might result in public concern.

12 Patenting human gene therapy

Among the new biotechnologies, human gene therapy has emerged as a potentially important tool for treating and preventing genetic diseases. Human gene therapy holds great promise for two primary reasons: (a) as a basic tool in biotechnology, it creates numerous scientific and technological possibilities involving gene transfer, and (b) because of its potential therapeutic applications, it hold great commercial promise with a significant economic impact. But its importance goes far beyond these possibilities. If adequately successful, it will revolutionize the medicine of the future and will have a profound impact on out moral and ethical outlook. Still further lies the world of positive eugenics which may finally become a reality, leading to a *Brave New World*, described by Aldous Huxley (1932) in his futuristic writings.

Consequently, it is not surprising that a great deal of attention has been paid to the development of more efficient techniques of gene transfer, especially from the viewpoint of treating or preventing such diseases as cancer, heart disease, AIDS, and various genetic diseases.

Therapy for ADA deficiency

The first disease to be successfully treated by gene therapy is adenosine deaminase deficiency (ADA). A pioneer in gene therapy, W. French Anderson, working with Eli Gilboa, engineered a series of vectors that could be used for gene transfer *in vivo*. One of these, containing the human ADA gene, was successfully used to correct the ADA deficiency of defective T and B cells from ADA (-) patients *in vitro*. Later, in monkeys, an autologous bone marrow transplantation/gene transfer protocol was established and expression of the human ADA gene in the bloodstream of several primates was demonstrated. Anderson then collaborated with S. Rosenberg and M. Blaese, to carry out the first approved human gene transfer/ therapy clinical protocols. At first, a marker gene was used to study adoptive immunotherapy for cancer, and it showed that gene transfer was safe and useful to elicit valuable scientific and clinical information (*New England Journal of Medicine*, August,

1990). The first human gene therapy protocol began on September 14, 1990, when a four-year girl was successfully treated for Severe Combined Immunodeficiency (SCID) which was caused by the absence of the enzyme adenosine deaminase (ADA). T lymphocytes were removed from the patient at intervals of one to several months, a normal ADA gene inserted into them by gene transfer, and the corrected cells were returned to her body. The patient's immune system gradually returned to normal and remains so until now. The success of this experiment has clearly established the emerging field of human gene therapy on a firm footing.

U.S. patent for gene therapy (# 5, 399, 346)

This patent was issued to W. French Anderson, R. Michael Blaese, and Steven A. Rosenberg, on March 21, 1995. The patent reads:

> This invention relates to the use of primary human cells as vehicles for human gene transfer. More particularly, this invention relates to the use of human cells (such as, for example, but not limited to, human blood cells) as vehicles for the transfer of human genes encoding therapeutic agents/or genes encoding detectable markers.

The patent emphasizes the suitability of lymphocytes to carry out experiments in gene insertion, gene expression and other properties of the gene-transduced cells. Because long-lived antigen specific memory lymphocytes proliferate when exposed to their appropriate antigen, the population of gene-treated lymphocytes can be selectively and specifically expanded in vivo by immunization of the host. Furthermore, some gene-treated antigen-specific lymphocytes can be used to deliver specific gene products directly to the site of pathology (e.g. tumor). Tumor infiltrating lymphocytes (TIL) transduced with genes promoting secretion of a recombinant cytokine and using the TIL's own unique antigen-specific receptors to direct them to tumor sites will result in greater antitumor effect with less toxicity.

The central feature of the claim is that primary human cells which are genetically engineered with DNA (RNA), encoding a therapeutic agent of interest, are employed as a therapeutic agent for the purpose of treatment and/or prophylaxis.

Recombinant DNA Advisory Committee (RAC)

The origins of RAC go back to 1973 when a committee of scientists was convened by the National Academy of Sciences under the chairmanship of molecular biologist Paul Berg. That committee recommended a moratorium on the cloning of genes for antibiotic resistance and of DNA from animal viruses until an international conference was convened to discuss these issues in detail. That conference was held at Asilomar, California, in 1975, and came to be known as the "Asilomar Conference" in the following years. That conference set in motion a series of steps which eventually led to the establishment of the Office of Recombinant DNA Activities (ORDA) and the Recombinant DNA Advisory committee (RAC) of the National Institutes of Health (NIH) in Bethesda, Maryland. Together, the function of ORDA and RAC is to meet the need for public participation in genetic research, and to ensure compliance with the NIH guidelines. During the past several years, ORDA served as a national focal point for information, providing advice to organizations, research institutions, biosafety committees, federal agencies, state and local governments, and the biotechnology industry.

The RAC held several meeting since 1975, establishing a set of guidelines for recombinant DNA research and revising them or updating them each year as new discoveries and new information came to light. The revised guidelines clearly established the responsibilities of the institutional biosafety committee, the principal investigator, the NIH, and the RAC. The guidelines and all major action were published in the *Federal Register*. Ethical and safety consideration always received special attention.

The first human gene transfer protocol was approved by the RAC and the NIH Director in 1988. Since its inception, the RAC had dealt with a number of emerging technologies. At first, many protocols using retroviral vectors were approved for treating a variety of malignancies, AIDS, and familial hypercholesterolemia, etc. Later on, the RAC has seen the emergence of protocols using non-retroviral vectors for gene transfer such as adenovirus vectors, liposomes, and microbalistic injection for the treatment of cancer, AIDS, and cystic fibrosis.

A number of applications are cited in the patent. The expression product of the DNA (RNA), which is used for transducing the human cells, may or may not be secreted from the cells. For instance, in the case of ADA, the expression product of DNA encoding ADA is not secreted from the cells. The human cells may also be genetically engineered with DNA (RNA) which encodes either a marker or therapeutic, the cells expressing the encoded product *in vivo*.

The invention is further directed to enhance the therapeutic effects of human primary cells, for instance, by enhancing the effects of those cells which specifically target to a tissue site in a patient (such as tumor infiltrating lymphocytes or TIL cells). In other cases, genetically engineered primary human cells may not be targeted to a specific site but may function as a systemic therapeutic, that is to say, a desired therapeutic agent can be expressed and secreted from the cells systemically.

In some instances, the primary human cells may be either primary human nucleated blood cells or primary human tumor cells. In the former case, the primary human blood cell may include leukocytes, granulocytes, monocytes, macrophages, lymphocytes, immature forms of each of the previous cells (as well as immature erythroblasts) (CD34 + cells) and totipotent stem cells.

The patent is a very broad one which includes any DNA having clinical usefulness, for example, any DNA that directly or indirectly enhances the therapeutic effects of the cells. Examples of DNA, which can be used for genetic engineering, include blood cells encoding cytokines such as tumor necrosis factor (TNF), interleukins (for example, interleukins 1-12), interferons, T-cell receptor proteins and the Fc receptors for antigen-binding domains of antibodies, such as immunoglobulins.

As mentioned earlier, genes may be inserted purely for marking purposes. Their function is mainly to facilitate determination of the traffic and survival of the transformed cells in vivo. Examples of such marker genes include the neomycin resistance (neoR) gene, multi-drug resistant gene, thymidine kinase gene, galactosidase, dehydrofolate reductase (DHFR) and chloroamphenicol acetyl transferase.

The cells may be genetically engineered *in vitro* or *in vivo*. Cells may be removed from a patient and after genetically engineered *in vitro* with DNA (RNA) encoding the therapeutic agent, they are readministered to the patient. This procedure is sometimes called an *ex vivo* treatment. On the other hand, DNA (RNA) encoding the therapeutic agent may be administered to the patient for delivery of the DNA *in vivo* to the targeted cells by the use of a variety of delivery systems such as a retroviral or other viral vector, or liposomes, etc. A pharmaceutically acceptable carrier bay be used for administration to a patient. Primary human nucleated blood cells may be administered either by using a liquid carried (e.g. saline solution) or a solid carrier (e.g. an implant). A liquid carrier containing the engineered cells may be introduced intravenously, subcutaneously, intramuscularly, intraperitoneally, or intralesionaly, etc.

Gene therapy for cardiovascular disease

The first clinical trial of gene therapy for cardiovascular disease was initiated in 1992 when a gene for the LDL receptor was introduced into the liver of a patient with familial hypercholesterolemia (1994). Since 1990 when the first clinical trial of gene therapy began (for ADA deficiency), the concept of gene therapy has become much broader, encompassing not only replacing a missing function in an inherited disorder, but also enhancing normal function, providing new therapeutic functions, or interfering with pathological functions associated with many common diseases (Ledley and Anderson, 1996). The following is a brief summary of some aspects of gene therapy applied to cardiovascular disease.

The aim of the first clinical trials of gene therapy was to lower cholesterol by introducing gene products altering cholesterol by introducing gene products altering cholesterol metabolism. There is evidence from animal experimentation which shows that expression of an LDL-receptor gene in LDL receptor-deficient rabbits, transgenic mice, and normal mice results in lowering of cholesterol (reviewed in Ledly and Anderson, 1996).

These are but a few of the important examples which indicate the increasing importance of human gene therapy and its potential applications. As it becomes more and more successful in treating or preventing various genetic disease, we can expect investigators and firms to file several new patent claims.

13 IPR in a north-south context

Technological and economic disparity between developed and developing countries has been pointed out by some as a possible reason for making certain exceptions for less developed countries with respect to the institution of intellectual property rights. Park and Ginarte (1996) have discussed this problem in terms of a *North-South* dialogue. They have used the term *North* in this context to refer to technology-producing countries and *South* to technology-importing countries. However, it is realized that not all technology-innovating countries are geographically located in the Northern Hemisphere nor all technology-importing countries are in the south. Nevertheless, the countries of the north tend to be wealthier and technologically innovative. It has been argued that because of the inability of southern countries to pay for the IPR-protected innovations, they may be denied access to innovations that are crucial to their social and economic progress. Some have even suggested that there are sound ethical arguments against restricting the flow of technology from the North to the South. Park and Ginarte (1996) have mentioned that much of the focus on international violations of IPR has so far centered on the "imitation" activities of the South. However, they have omitted to mention that countries of the South have been exploited for centuries, first by colonial rulers (mostly from the North) and later by big multinational companies (also from the North), who paid no compensation whatsoever. Needless to say, their exploitations were not bound by any internationally agreed convention. Their main motivation has been economic greed, not international law. Park and Ginarte (1996) have also omitted any discussion of the need for compensating indigenous peoples and tribal communities of various nations of the South for their traditional knowledge and resources that have been exploited and stolen (often under the threat of violence by foreign armies). Quite often, the exploiters are from the Northern Hemisphere. Surely, any meaningful North-South economic dialogue must take a comprehensive view of all these factors!

The usual arguments have been advanced by Park and Ginarte (1996) for a universal IPR protection, such as IPR providing a strong incentive for research and development and so on. However, one may not agree with their statement that "lagging economic development is a consequence . . . of weak IPR". That may be so in some countries, but this is a complicated situation. There are historical factors which should be taken into consideration. Are we referring to the intellectual property rights of indigenous people of the countries of the South or of the multinational companies or rich countries of the North? Surely, we must recognize the rights of both southern and northern countries.

It is well known that, in the economic context, private interests are not often compatible with social interests or even what is considered to be common good. The innovator is typically interested only in the costs and benefits of his R & D investment, but not to the entire society. One may extend this principle universally to understand the attitude of large corporations towards the countries of the South.

Time-consistency has been mentioned as an important factor in maintaining sound North-South relations. A strong and credible IPR system will encourage a steady flow of foreign technology transfer. Any deviation from that policy will be costly because it will take longer time to reestablish a smooth transfer of foreign technology. Poor IPR protection in countries of the Southern Hemisphere has been mentioned as a factor in discouraging further investment in R & D by the countries of the North. This situation is further complicated when an imitated product from the South is reexported back to its country of origin in the North, thereby undercutting the profits that are expected to result from the original investment. On the other hand, exporting manufactured products to the countries of the South from Northern countries, which utilize raw material of the South while paying no just compensation for those naturally occurring materials and knowledge, raises serious ethical questions.

IPR and developing countries

Park and Ginarte (1996) have also considered certain cultural attitudes in the South which may impact on the success of IPR implementation. Historically, some countries of the South (such as South Korea) have regarded new ideas and technologies as "public goods", which should be shared freely by all members of the community. Cultural pride takes precedence over incentive for private benefits. There is also the widespread belief in countries that IPR system could be modified to suit a particular country's specific needs. Nevertheless, Park and Ginarte (1996) believe that protecting IPR is clearly in the interests of the less developed countries. They argue that while tariffs are barriers to international trade, social intervention in the form of IPR promotes the market for innovations. However, their view that mismanaged monetary and technology policies of the South are solely to be blamed for the technological backwardness of the South may seem too simplistic and naive because it ignores the historical realities of commercial exploitation of the developing world. Surely, rich and consuming nations have significantly contributed to the increasing depletion of natural resources and diminishing biodiversity far more than the less developed countries of the South. It is increasingly clear that many developing nations are keenly aware of the need to protect their biodiversity and the role played by intellectual property rights in achieving that goal.

Developing countries

Evenson (1993) compared the IPR situation in six types of developing countries which are at different stages of economic development. Developing countries include traditional economies, others which are nearing newly industrialized status (NICs), and a few others which are approaching the threshold of global technological competitiveness. Basically, the two stages of development recognized by Evenson (1993) are: (1) emerging islands of modernization, and (2) others struggling for mobilization and mastery. Most of the countries in stage 1 do not have adequate personnel or the necessary legal system to administer IPR laws as required under the GATT regulations. Stage 2 countries include several which have displayed impressive industrial growth, including some recently industrialized Mediterranean countries such as Spain. Stage 1 countries have no industrial R & D capacity and their public sector is underdeveloped. On the other hand, private sector R & D is acquiring a new importance in the Stage 2 countries. These include many NICs (newly industrialized countries) which spend about 1 percent of their industrial output on R & D, which is less than both the OECD standard of 2+ percent as well as the standard of the recently industrialized Mediterranean countries. Most of the Stage 1 countries make no investment in science R & D, whereas those of Stage 2 group make small investments in science and technology.

Evenson (1993) argued that, in practice, the international IPR regulations have not worked well for any of the developing countries because they do not have exporters' interests to protect. They have no rights to protect in foreign countries. It

Table 13.1 Countries at varying stages of scientific and technological development

Technology Class	Asia and Near East	Latin America and Caribbean	Sub-Saharan Africa
Stage 1. Emerging Countries of Modernization			
Traditional technology	Yemen, Laos	Surinam	Guinea
First emergence	Nepal, Papua New Guinea	Haiti, Guyana	Ethiopia, Burkina Faso
Island of modernization	Sri Lanka Tunisia Indonesia	Jamaica Peru	Kenya Ivory Coast Zimbabwe
Stage 2. Struggling for Mobilization and Mastery			
Master of conventional technology	Iran Malaysia Turkey	Colombia Argentina	
NICs	India Thailand Hong Kong	Mexico	South Africa
Threshold of technological competitiveness	Singapore Taiwan South Korea	Brazil	

Source: Evenson (1993)

has been suggested that developing countries have allowed conflict over the terms of importing technology to overshadow the strengthening of domestic innovation and IPR protection. They have yet to use IPR as their major policy tools in international trade. It is also not clear if the willingness of foreign technology suppliers to provide technology to developing countries is improved by stronger IPRs.

U.S. - India Science and Technology Pact

A draft of the U.S.- India Science and Technology Pact was circulated among the leaders of both countries in 1994, shortly before the visit of Prime Minister P.V. Narasimha Rao to Washington, D.C. However, that proposed agreement was never finalized and signed by the leaders of both countries because no agreement could be reached concerning the wording of the clause II (B) 2 (b).

AGREEMENT BETWEEN
THE GOVERNMENT OF THE UNITED STATES OF AMERICA
AND
THE GOVERNMENT OF THE REPUBLIC OF INDIA
ON COOPERATION IN SCIENCE AND TECHNOLOGY

The Government of the United States of America and the Government of the Republic of India (hereinafter referred to as the Parties):

Aware of the contribution that effective scientific and technological cooperation can make, not only in advancing world frontiers in science and technology, but also in enhancing the development of human and economic resources of both countries;

Recognizing the scientific accomplishments realized under the 1983 Science and Technology Initiative, the 1987 Agreement Between the Government of the United States of America and the Government of the Republic of India on Educational, Cultural, and Scientific Cooperation, and other collaborative agreements; and

Reaffirming the benefits of science and technology to Indo-U.S. bilateral relations;

Have agreed as follows:

Article I

The principle objective of this Agreement is to facilitate broad opportunities for cooperation in scientific and technological fields of mutual interest, thereby promoting the progress of science and technology for the benefit of both countries and of mankind.

Article II

Cooperation under this Agreement may be undertaken in the fields of agriculture, non-nuclear energy, health and medical sciences, biology, environment and ecology, atmospheric and marine research information science physical, chemical and material sciences, metrology and standards, earth science, heritage protection, and such other areas of science and technology as may be mutually agreed. Activities may include the exchange of scientific and technological information, joint conduct of research projects, exchanges of scientists and technical experts, convening of seminars and meetings, and other forms of scientific and technological cooperation as may be mutually agreed.

Article III
The Parties shall encourage the development of cooperation between government agencies and institutions, universities, and other entities in both countries.

Article IV
A. Specific arrangements implementing this Agreement may cover administrative arrangements, funding, and other appropriate matters. Unless otherwise provided for in an implementing arrangement, each Party or participating entity shall bear the cost of its participation and that of its personnel in cooperation activities under this Agreement.

B. Except as otherwise provided in arrangements implementing this Agreement, protection of intellectual property and rights thereto will be as set forth in Annex I, which forms an integral part of this Agreement.

Article V
Cooperation under this Agreement shall be subject to the laws and regulations in each country. All cooperative activities under this Agreement shall be subject to the availability of funds.

Article VI
Each Party shall, with respect to cooperative activities under this Agreement, facilitate prompt entry into and exit from its territory of equipment, research vessels and personnel of the other Party, and also provide access to relevant geographic areas, institutions, data and materials. Such access shall be in accordance with the generally accepted international principles and practice.

Article VII
Scientific and technological information derived from cooperative activities under this Agreement should be made available to the scientific community through customary channels, in accordance with the normal procedures of the participating entities and to the extent consistent with Annex I and implementing arrangements.

Article VIII
Scientists, technical experts, and entities of third countries or international organizations may be invited, with the consent of both Parties, or their implementing entities, as appropriate, to participate in the projects and programs being carried out under this Agreement.

Article IX
A. A U.S.-India joint board shall be established which shall adopt procedures for its operation, and shall meet as mutually agreed, alternately in the United States and in India.
B. The Joint Board shall review, assess, facilitate, and make specific recommendations concerning scientific and technical cooperation.
C. To carry out its functions, the Joint Board may when necessary create subcommittees or working groups.
D. To assist the Joint Board, each Party shall designate an Executive Agent. The Executive Agent of the United States shall be the Department of State, Bureau of Oceans and International Environmental and Scientific Affairs, Office of Cooperative Programs; and of the Republic of India, the Department of Science and Technology. The Executive Agents shall cooperate to expedite the approval process of proposed projects and promote rapid implementation of approved activities and programs.

Article X
This Agreement is without prejudice to cooperation which may be undertaken pursuant to other arrangements between the Parties.

Article XI
A. This Agreement shall enter into force upon signature and shall remain in force for five years. It may be amended or extended by written agreement of the Parties. It may be terminated by either Party upon six months written notice.
B. The termination of this Agreement shall not affect the validity or duration of any implementing arrangements made under it.

DONE at _____, this ___ day of _____, in duplicate, in the English language.

FOR THE GOVERNMENT OF THE
UNITED STATES OF AMERICA

FOR THE GOVERNMENT OF THE
REPUBLIC OF INDIA

ANNEX I – INTELLECTUAL PROPERTY

Pursuant to Article V of this Agreement;

The Parties shall ensure adequate and effective protection of intellectual property created or furnished under this Agreement and relevant implementing arrangements. The Parties agree to notify one another in a timely fashion of any inventions or copyrighted works arising under this Agreement and to seek protection for such intellectual property in a timely fashion. Rights to such intellectual property shall be allocated as provided in this Annex.

I. SCOPE

A. This Annex is applicable to all cooperative activities undertaken pursuant to this Agreement, except as otherwise specifically agreed by the Parties or their designees.
B. For the purposes of this Agreement, "intellectual property" shall have the meaning found in Article 2 of the Convention Establishing the World Intellectual Property Organization, done at Stockholm, July 14, 1967.
C. This Annex addresses the allocation of rights, interests, and royalties between the Parties. Each Party shall ensure that the other Party can obtain the rights to intellectual property allocated in accordance with the Annex, by obtaining those rights from its own participants through contracts or other legal means, if necessary. This Annex does not otherwise alter or prejudice the allocation between a Party and its nationals, which shall be determined by that Party's laws and practices.
D. Disputes concerning intellectual property arising under this Agreement should be resolved through discussion between the concerned participating institutions or, if necessary, the Parties or their designees. Upon mutual agreement of the Parties, a dispute shall be submitted to an arbitrary tribunal for binding arbitration in accordance with the applicable rules of international law. Unless the Parties or their designees agree otherwise in writing, the arbitration rules of UNCITRAL shall govern.
E. Termination or expiration of this Agreement shall not affect rights or obligations under this Annex.
F. Cooperative activities will not be entered into:
    1. where there is a reasonable prospect, as determined by either Party, of producing inventions in areas not considered patentable subject matter by both Parties; or

2. in the area of semiconductor mask works until such works are considered protectable by both Parties.

G. In the event that either Party believes that a particular joint research project under this Agreement will lead to the creation or furnishing of intellectual property of a type not protected by the applicable laws of one of the Parties, the Parties shall immediately hold discussions to implement the provisions of IIB2b. The joint activities in question will be suspended during the discussions. If no agreement can be reached within a three month period from the date of the request for discussions, the Parties shall cease the cooperation in the project in question.

II. ALLOCATION OF RIGHTS

A. Each party shall be entitled to a non-exclusive, irrevocable, royalty-free license in all countries to translate, reproduce, and publicly distribute scientific and technical journal articles, reports, and books directly arising from cooperation under this Agreement. All publicly distributed copies of a copyrighted work prepared under this provision shall indicate the names of the authors of the work unless an author explicitly declines to be named.

B. Rights to all forms of intellectual property other than those rights described in Section II[A] above, shall be allocated as follows:

1. Visiting researchers, for example, scientists visiting primarily in furtherance of their education, shall receive intellectual property rights under the policies of the host institution. In addition, each visiting researcher named as an inventor shall be entitled to share in a portion of any royalties earned by the host institution from the licensing of such intellectual property.

2. [a] For intellectual property created during joint research, for example, when the Parties, participating institutions, or participating personnel have agreed in advance on the scope of work, each Party shall be entitled to obtain all rights and interests in its own territory. Rights and interests in third countries will be determined in implementing arrangements. If research is not designated as "joint research" in the relevant implementing arrangement, rights to intellectual property arising from the research will be allocated in accordance with paragraph IIB1. In addition, each person named as inventor shall be entitled to share in a portion of any royalties earned by either institution from the licensing of the property.

[b] notwithstanding paragraph IIB2 [a], if a type of intellectual property is available under the laws of one Party but not the other Party, the Party whose laws provide for this type of protection shall be entitled to all rights and interests

worldwide. Persons named as inventors of the property shall nonetheless be entitled to royalties as provided in paragraph IIB2 [a].

III. BUSINESS-CONFIDENTIAL INFORMATION

In the event that information identified in a timely fashion as business-confidential is furnished or created under the Agreement, each Party and its participants shall protect such information in accordance with applicable laws, regulations, and administrative practice. Information may be identified as "business-confidential" if a person having the information may derive an economic benefit from it or may obtain a competitive advantage over those who do not have it, the information is generally not known or publicly available from other sources, and the owner has not previously made the information available without imposing in a timely manner an obligation to keep it confidential.

IV. TECHNOLOGY TRANSFER

A. Both parties agree that no information or equipment requiring protection in the interests of national defense or foreign relations of either Party and classified in accordance with the applicable national laws and regulations shall be provided under this Agreement. In the event that information or equipment which is known or believed to require such protection is identified in the course of cooperative activities undertaken pursuant to this Agreement, it shall be brought immediately to the attention of the appropriate officials and the Parties shall consult to identify appropriate security measures to be agreed upon by the Parties in writing and applied to this information and equipment and shall, if appropriate, amend this Agreement to incorporate such measures.

B. The transfer of unclassified export-controlled information or equipment between the Parties shall be in accordance with the relevant laws and regulations of each Party. If either Party deems it necessary, detailed provisions for the prevention of unauthorized transfer or retransfer of such information or equipment shall be incorporated into the contracts or implementing arrangements. Export controlled information shall be marked to identify it as export controlled and identify any restrictions on further use or transfer.

14 Is a uniform IPR system necessary?

Sherwood (1993) and others have argued in favor of a uniform IPR system for the entire world. In order to have an enforceable IPR system, one must also have an appropriate judiciary and a bureaucracy that administers the system fairly and efficiently. Without an efficient infrastructure, it is doubtful whether a meaningful IPR system can be enforced throughout the world. However, the specific intellectual property systems of different countries need not be identical. It is not necessary to harmonize the laws, procedures, and regulations in every country. The assurance that others can be prevented from unauthorized copying has been shown to be a powerful stimulus to the process of invention, technical advancement, and creative expression. The knowledge that an inventor's efforts can be safeguarded from misappropriation, no matter which country becomes the center of their activity, provides a highly simulative global system.

The intellectual property systems of various countries have been rated on a scale of 1 to 100–for instance, Germany at about 90, the U.S. and some of the European countries in the high 80s, Mexico at 75, and Argentina and Brazil only in the 30s and 40s. Sherwood (1993) suggested that only when a system rises above 70 will it produce significant results. These results can be measured in following terms: (a) private venture capital firms become more willing to invest in technology-based start-up companies, (b) valuable technical knowledge flows more readily from university laboratories to the marketplace, and (c) local firms become willing to invest a substantial share of their resources to internal research.

Two examples have been cited where, despite some fundamental differences in the legal systems and other aspects, congruence in the IPR systems has been achieved. These are (a) the various national intellectual property systems of the European community which have not been harmonized, yet trade between member countries has flourished, and (b) the individual states in the U.S.A where interstate business continues in spite of profound differences in local laws and taxation systems.

Any international system of agreement must be flexible enough to readily accommodate new forms of technology. Recent years have seen the rapid growth of both biotechnology and computer software. No doubt some countries are able to lead others in developing and incorporating new technologies. A uniform intellectual property system would have three distinct characteristics: (a) all forms of intellectual property would be included, (b) each would have efficient public administration, and (c) each would have the appropriate judicial system to enforce individual rights. Sherwood (1993) argued that the benefits of an international congruent intellectual property system would benefit all countries, no matter what their stage of development may be.

Free riding has been discussed in relation to intellectual property rights. This situation arises when a country with no system of intellectual property rights allows its citizens to take the technical knowledge of another country which recognizes the intellectual property rights of its citizens. From a short-term point of view, free riding may seem to be beneficial for a few companies. However, it has been argued that, in the long-term, it diminishes incentive for innovation and development. It is obvious that many modern technologies cannot be transferred without the active cooperation of the host country. For the receiving country, free riding may result in the loss of opportunities in innovative research, development of new technologies, and in creating new jobs and prosperity. It has been suggested further that copying products is not equivalent to the acquisition of technology. For instance, software, and medicine are easy to copy in most instances, but the underlying technology is too complex to be readily transferred to a developing country (Sherwood, 1993). It must also be emphasized that developing countries vary greatly in their degree of developing and technological capacity. Some have become exporting countries in selected technologies. For instance, the software industry of India has been supplying the software needs of many U.S. companies in recent years. Many so-called developing countries now trade in technologies with each other at a much lower cost than would be the case with a developed country.

There is a growing awareness in the developing countries to institute a sound intellectual property protection. Quite often, when individuals from the developing nations, who are trained abroad, return home to pursue innovative research they are reluctant to do so without the protection of a secure intellectual property system. Sherwood (1993) mentioned the case of a Brazilian scientist who has made significant medical inventions, but since Brazil excludes pharmaceuticals from patent protection, he used to fly to Europe to file his patent claims. Another Brazilian example involved a professor from the University of Sao Paulo who is the joint inventor of a bacterium that efficiently produces ethanol from sugar waste. The Brazilian professor (and two American colleagues) were granted a U.S. patent while he was a visiting professor at the University of Florida. However, in spite of its extensive sugar crops, Brazil is not a beneficiary from this invention. Its laws would not grant a patent of that kind.

A similar situation exists in India where patenting of living cells, tissues, and organisms is not possible under the existing laws. If a Indian scientist were to invent a unique organism, he (or she) would have to file his patent claim in a foreign country where such claims are recognized, licensed and protected. Coffee growers and cut-flower growers association of Colombia faced similar frustrations and are reluctant to pursue innovative research programs when no protection is available. Furthermore, it discourages foreign growers and companies from exporting novel breeding stocks to Colombia which does not offer protection for their unique resources.

Problems in international cooperation

It is clear that if a congruent world intellectual property system were to be successfully instituted it would provide a powerful stimulus to the global economy. It would lead to increased international cooperation in research and development, innovative programs, and also hopefully increased transfer of technology between nations, leading to greater prosperity and employment. However, many practical problems need to be overcome before such an ideal state of affairs can be achieved.

First, a primary obstacle is the overwhelming fear of many developing nations that the IPR system is designed solely to benefit the developed countries at the expense of the developing countries.

Second, the legal and administrative infrastructure required for instituting a universal IPR system is simply beyond the resources of many developing countries.

Third, the increased tariffs incorporating the profit system of western countries would be prohibitively expensive for many developing countries.

Fourth, some believe that the IPR system would enable large multinational companies to destroy fledgling industries of the developing countries.

Fifth, past experience indicates that exploitation of natural resources of the developing countries (e.g. medicinal plants) by the developed countries has led to the depletion of several species which now face extinction.

Sixth, there are inadequate measures to compensate indigenous tribes and farmers in the developing countries who preserved traditional knowledge and biological resources for centuries. Such knowledge has been commercially exploited by the developed countries, at first under colonial rule and later through the multinational companies. Yet, no systematic program of compensation has been initiated to date. However, note the account of the program initiated by the U.S. National Cancer Institute which is grossly inadequate to address this problem at present and does not include any plan to compensate for past exploitation. Surely, both the U.S. and the countries of western Europe should consider this issue very seriously.

This situation is typical of all recent discussions which support a universal IPR system. No mention is made of past exploitation of the resources of the developing nations, let alone compensating them in some fashion. Inadequacy of compensation is the hallmark also of all discussions which involve the utilization of traditional knowledge and conservation methods which have preserved such biological resources as the crop germplasms and the utilization of medicinal herbs.

It has been argued by some that an upgrading of the quality of research in all fields of endeavor is essential before instituting a strong IPR system. It can be argued with equal emphasis that a weak IPR protection would slow down the process of achieving a higher level of research and development. The fundamental question is not whether a country ought to have IPR protection for its inventions but the type of protection needed to safeguard its property and if the protection is strong enough to eliminate exploitation of its resources by bigger and richer countries. A basic problem is to not just to have an IPR system on paper but to follow the IPR regulations in practice to the fullest extent possible. It should be backed up by an efficient judicial system that is fair, impartial and incorruptible.

Today there is hardly any country which does not take its IPR seriously. Most have either instituted the IPR system already or are in the process of doing so. But no matter what the size of the country or its economic status may be, no country likes to be pressured by any foreign country about its IPR policy. Much of the world's activity is driven by technology and commerce. Ideology seems to play a secondary role.

Global activity

It has been suggested by Armstrong (1993) and others that the best reason for globalizing intellectual property systems is because research, development, and invention are all increasingly becoming international activities. Countries with weak intellectual property systems tend to receive less technical knowledge because: (a) first, even if proprietary knowledge is copied, those who obtain such knowledge do not have access to associated knowledge or the active cooperation of the unwilling source; (b) second, countries with weak intellectual property systems lack the infrastructure necessary for building a strong technological base and are hindered from developing a strong team of technical personnel who can lead the country or train younger people; and (c) it would be difficult for countries with weak intellectual property systems to engage in vigorous trade in "pirated" products, especially with countries having strong protective systems. Such a situation would not be conducive to foreign investment which is urgently needed in many developing countries.

The most serious consequence of a weak intellectual property system is the lack of opportunities for participating in the latest global activities in science and technology. High level scientific research is the key to technology development and eventually economic success. Some recent examples are high-temperature superconductivity, genetic engineering, and high speed computer technology. New technologies tend to displace entire industries. What was commonly practiced yesterday is outdated today. This process of rapid change invariably includes a great need for public education. This is especially true of the legal profession and the associated administrative bureaucracy which would be entrusted with the responsibility of overseeing the IPR systems in practice.

Infrastructure

India clearly stands as the outstanding example where progress is being held back because the modernization of its infrastructure has not kept pace with its economic liberalization policies. There are glaring deficiencies in all aspects of India's infrastructure which are at variance with other, more progressive aspects of its development. On the one hand, we have well developed and liberal educational institutions which use English language as the medium of instruction, a large educated and consumer-oriented middle class, and a democratic form of centralized government with liberal policy toward foreign investment. On the other hand, communication and transportation systems are still very poor (at least fifty years behind modern times judging from the per capita number of telephones and automobiles–two basic needs), one of the lowest standards of public sanitation in the world, unchecked population growth and highly polluted cities. Poor environmental quality is one of the reasons for periodic epidemics and public health crises of various kinds. Added to these problems is the outdated administrative bureaucracy, (a colonial vestige!), which tends to discourage foreign investment. Is it any wonder that economic progress is at a snail's pace when compared to several other countries of southeast Asia?

To be fair, these contradictions are the natural result when a country–long steeped in traditional customs and beliefs for centuries–is struggling to acquire 21st century technology and join the family of nations many of which have a far more developed technological infrastructure. Surely, this stage of economic progress is characteristic of all developing countries which share a similar historical past. But India's large growing population, its sheer size and its geopolitical situation greatly increase the stress and strains of these internal contradictions.

Armstrong (1993) emphasized three trends in global developments in science and technology that are relevant in shaping IPR systems in the international context.

(a) First, science continues to produce surprises, so any system that is devised should be able to absorb and cope with new developments of the highest order, including the rapid conversion of new scientific advances into products and services for practical use. The basic legal infrastructure which has served will in the past for patent protection should be used, with some flexibility, to readily cope with new technologies. However, Armstrong (1993) argued that the existing IPR systems should continue to be used rather than devise new exotic mechanisms of protection.

(b) The second point is the great diversity of ever expanding topics which scientific research brings forth and the global nature of research conducted by private firms. To keep pace with the expanding opportunities in technology many large companies devote a significant portion of their R & D budgets to develop collaborative projects with smaller firms. Armstrong (1993) suggested that this situation provides an opportunity for smaller firms in developing countries to enter into collaborative arrangements with large multinational companies. But unless they have adequate intellectual property protection they would not be able to find large companies which would be willing to collaborate with them.

The great diversity of research collaborations and the institutions involved include universities, national laboratories, federal and state-funded research programs, corporate research programs, research conducted under contracts, and smaller private research groups and individuals. There are other cooperative alliances which operate at great distances from each other, either in the same country or in distant countries. On-line computer-connected cooperation is also becoming more frequent in research collaboration. Research alliances, specialist groups, circulated newsletters, E-mail communication in selected groups and other forms of communication have increase the pace of communication and technological change. They have led to increasing research collaboration on a global scale. Global networks have now become commonplace in research among university teams, large and small firms, and state-funded research. A well known example is the availability of software programmers in India through satellite links. The same is true of various collaborating teams in the entertainment industry from different countries via satellite links. Government share of research expenditure is declining in many countries. Consequently, private sector will be playing an increasing role in R & D. IPR issues will play a crucial role in attracting private funding and investing in research.

(c) Third, competitive advantage in any industry depends on frequent incremental refinements in technology which leads to shorter product lives. Also there is great pressure to diminish the time needed for scientific invention to reach the product application stage. Under the pressure of competition, new products appear continuously in the market place. Intellectual property systems must be able to distinguish between genuinely new products and imitations. The concept of patent law must also be able to distinguish between a basic invention and its subsequent improvements.

In contrast to the usual IPR protection, trade secrets are not created by a bureaucracy. Trade secret protection can be used for incremental advances. It is especially appropriate for process technology.

Global liberalism or monopoly?

Under the provisions of the *World Trade Organization* (WTO-Uruguay Round), dramatic changes are taking place to protect trade-related-intellectual-property rights (TRIPS). It was meant to create a global open-market economy with the stated purpose of reducing "distortions and impediments to international trade . . . and promote effective and adequate protection of intellectual property". Burch (1995) had suggested that the agreement is also a statement of "political principles described generally as liberal (in the sense of an ideology or worldview rather than as a partisan political label), and its comprehensive character hints at a nascent global culture or liberalism". According to this interpretation, WTO-TRIPS formalizes the global economy as a relatively open market requiring countries to conduct international trade in accordance with certain principles. These principles include private rights, "individual" rights, and exclusive rights–"rights to fair and equitable procedure" and rights to due process (WTO, 1995). According to Burch (1995), this agreement is applied globally and thematically to address political, economic, social, legal organizational, industrial, agricultural, and scientific concerns. By "liberalism", Burch (1995) was referring to an "outlook on social relations that attempts to balance individual freedoms against community interests, while minimizing the power of the state (Rapaczynski, 1987)".

Burch's (1995) argument may be outlined in the following steps:

(a) WTO-TRIPS is significantly an international property rights document.

(b) Exclusive, private property rights serve to define liberalism and liberal social life.

(c) Liberalism, in organizing social life in terms of the defining concepts, rights and property, constitutes a particular pattern of social relations.

(d) The particular pattern manifest by liberalism is a culture, understood as a way of life or a set of meanings and under-standings by which people understand themselves and their world, as well as behave in, make sense of, and evaluate the world.

Burch (1995) envisioned a world of numerous conflicts–conflicts arising form a clash of liberal values with local norms. Examples cited by the author include Eastern Europe and China. He mentions pirated software, compact discs, and light industrial products as evidence of selective adherence to global rules. Burch stated that seemingly neutral rules may foster self-serving outcomes; although the U.S. and British governments condemn pirating by some countries, yet American and British firms engaged in extensive "reverse engineering" and "industrial espionage" for many decades (Chernow, 1990; Kurth, 1979).

In this context, Burch (1995) explained his idea of "liberalism" in the following manner: "Liberals think habitually and effortlessly in terms legal and economic concepts and in terms of property and rights. Such reckonings are hallmark of the modern world". He noted that the first world economies are expected to grow at a modest 2.7 per cent in the next decade, whereas the south and east Asian economies are expected to grow at the rate of 5.3 to 7.6 per cent. The large industrializing economies of China, India, Indonesia, and Thailand are expected to continue their rapid expansions. Under these circumstances, Burch (1995) considered that the heightened role of IPR in international trade is a timely necessity.

Human cost

Quite understandably, there are several other points of view. In contrast to Burch's optimistic liberal interpretation, economist and social scientist Noam Chomsky stated that hidden human cost and monopoly by the developed nations with great clout and resources would lead to disaster. Developing nations would be trapped in a situation of no progress.

Chomsky (1996) wrote:

> GATT is called a free trade agreement, just as NAFTA was, but that's nonsense. These things are not about free trade and they're certainly not agreements. In fact, most of the people in the world are opposed to them. Intellectual property rights have to do with protectionism. The US, and in fact the rich countries generally, have led the insistence that the GATT agreement, like NAFTA [North American Free Trade Agreement], include strong intellectual property rights. That's protectionism. That means increasing the power of patents. Patents are protectionist devices.

Chomsky wrote that patents are designed to insure that the technology of the future is in the hands of transnational corporations and they want to be publicly subsidized in research and development.

India

With special reference to India, Chomsky (1996) wrote:

> India has a big pharmaceutical industry. It can produce drugs at a fraction of the cost of what Merck would like to price to sell. In fact, drug prices are way lower in India than in Pakistan next door because India happened to develop its own pharmaceutical industry. The American corporations don't like that. . . . They want more profit, which means more children die in India. They want to make sure that India doesn't produce drugs at less than the cost of American drugs.

According to Chomsky, this is achieved in two ways under GATT. One way is to increase the length of patents. The other is to change their character from process patents to product patents. Under the new rules, if Merck figures out a certain way to produce a drug they can hold that patent for 20 years because it is a product. They can hold the process for another 20 years. Chomsky cited a recent report that India had finally agreed to liberalize their pharmaceutical industry. He concluded that the result would be greatly increased drug prices and increased number of children's deaths, but more profits for western corporations.

With respect to agriculture, Chomsky wrote that heavily subsidized agri-business, which proved to be efficient in the western countries, would not be suitable for developing nations. This fact was also emphasized by others such as M.S. Swaminathan of India. That would lead to the unemployment of millions of peasants in the developing world. They would move to the cities causing chaos and widespread starvation. But, human cost of the developing nations is not a concern of the multinationals whose main interest is profit-driven. Concerning the rights of indigenous farmers and tribal people of the developing countries, Chomsky wrote:

> For thousands of years people in the south have been developing crops. They don't own them. They don't get any rights from that. . . . they have the rich gene pool and the thousands of years of experience in creating hybrids and figuring out what herb works. Then western corporation go in and take it for nothing. . . . We minimally modify it and sell it to them. We patent it. It is a scam designed to rob the poor and enrich the rich, like most social policy . . . The people who make social policy make it in their interest. They wouldn't be in a position to make social policy if they weren't rich and privileged. People suffer.

While Chomsky's cynicism is shared by many in the developing countries, it is also true that since the Uruguay Round many developing countries are increasingly aware of the inequities of international trade and tariffs. There is heightened concern about the rapidly disappearing resources of the third world. New conservation plans are being designed to correct this problem in various countries as well as under the auspices of the United Nations. In a discussion of the role of technology blending in development, Umberto Colombo (1991) wrote that it is the blend of new and traditional technologies that must be appropriate to a specific application, rather than any single one of them. He wrote: "Developing countries must devise new strategies for mobilizing their all too scarce resources, to promote endogenous, sustainable development". Third world societies will have to be prepared to assimilate innovation and not be dominated by it, especially in the initial stages of technology transfer.

15 Ethical issues in transfer of technology

Transfer of technology is rarely unidirectional. It is a two-way street. Just as the developing countries continue to benefit from the technology of western countries, the developed countries (especially the U.S.A.) continue to depend on the traditional knowledge and natural resources of the developing countries. There has been a tendency to protect the flow of technology from the developed countries to the developing nations, but not in the reverse direction. Evenson (1993) had pointed out that the developing countries will soon establish their own special brand of protection.

There are a number of ethical and moral questions which have emerged from our experience involving the transfer of technology:

(a) There is an inherent lack of fairness in instituting a global system which is easily affordable for the developed nations but is clearly an economic burden for many countries of Asia and Africa.

(b) Export of advanced technology to countries which lack adequately trained personnel or equipment to provide safeguards or screening methods may result in the adverse impact of new technologies on the environment and the ecology of the region. For instance, introduction of new recombinant genetic material or contamination by new viral or bacterial variants may lead to the destruction of indigenous varieties of plant and animal species.

(c) A number of serious ethical questions arise when technology transfer and IPR systems lead to the extinction of rare species, as in the case of medicinal plants.

(d) Export of technology to some countries may lead to the destruction of indigenous industries and disruption of local culture.

(e) Export of certain technologies, e.g. genetic engineering or transgenic technology, may pose ethical dilemmas because of their incompatibility with traditional religions and social customs. They may also pose a health threat to the human populations of the region.

(f) New technologies may lead to increased unemployment in a population unless accompanied by an appropriate training program and economic infra-structure.

(g) Withholding of patented biotechnology and medical information may lead to increased number of fetal and infant deaths (an other mortality) in the developing countries.

(h) Similar mortality may also result form the export of inadequately tested drugs and contaminated foods.

(i) Ethical issues are also involved when copyright infringement takes place and pirating of products becomes a common practice in some countries.

(j) Ethical and moral questions arise when rich and powerful nations exploit indigenous communities and traditional knowledge (as in the case of herbal medicine) of developing nations but provide inadequate or no compensation.

(k) Ethical question are clearly involved when rare species of medicinal plants are being depleted but no attempts are made at conservation.

Reductionism and intellectual property rights

Another point of view regarding the patenting of genes and the concept of intellectual property rights (IPR) was presented by Shiva (1995), especially with reference to the developing nations (formerly the third world countries). The views of this group are best illustrated by the following excerpts:

> Biodiversity has been redefined as 'biotechnological inventions' and living organisms have been redefined as 'gene constructs' to make the patenting of life forms appear less controversial . . . one characteristic of reductionist biology is to declare organisms and their functions as useless, simply on the basis of ignorance of their structure and function. Thus, crops and trees are declared 'weed,' forests 'scrub' and cattle breeds 'mongrel'; and DNA whose role is not understood is called junk DNA.

According to this unusual view, which tends to be a combination of feminist and eco-centric doctrines,

> patents encourage two forms of violence against living organisms: (1) they are linked to the manipulation of organisms as if they were machines, thus denying their innate self-organizing capacity; and (2) to permit patenting of future generations of life forms denies the self-reproducing capacity of living organisms.

This does not agree with the known principles of biology. On the contrary, patenting of life forms implies a recognition of the self-reproducing capacity of living organisms. Otherwise, patenting itself would be a futile exercise because it would have no future. Secondly, although it is possible to manipulate the genetic material with great skill, it is also recognized that the genome does not operate in a vacuum but it does interact with the environment, both within the cell as well as outside.

The biological views of this group do not seem to be founded on what we know of biology today. Its adherents seem to consider only isolated bits of knowledge that seem to justify whatever view they wish to promote.

It is a grossly misleading view that a "democracy" of life can be maintained while harnessing living organisms for food production and other purposes which have sustained our existence on this planet for several thousands of years. It is also misleading to believe that genetic engineering would necessarily lead to a reduction in biodiversity. On the contrary, genetic engineering could lead to a discovery of new forms of genetic recombination, which would increase genetic diversity. It is also true that most biologists and geneticists realize that a sound program of genetic engineering requires the maintenance of genetic diversity because a larger gene pool would be able to provide a greater opportunity for selection of desired genotypes and genetic engineering in the desired direction.

Under the feminist-ecological perspective, every aspect of biology assumes a political meaning which seems to bear no resemblance to the known facts of biology. It is a strange mix of science, politics, and sociology which tends to obscure the scientific content of a program. Consequently, the resulting message is garbled and out of focus. One wonders what the goal of such an approach might be and what purpose it would all serve. It is also an exaggeration to say that all scientists and all scientific policies are necessarily anti-feminist and anti-ecology.

Nature, technology and boundaries

A major contention of this group is that the traditional boundaries between various entities are breaking down. Barriers between species, barriers between the living and the non-living, and barriers between plant life and animal species are disappearing because of the application of genetic engineering and the transgenic technology. Relocation of the essence of life (whatever that may mean) has shifted to the level of the gene (or the DNA molecule) instead of the organism, or the species, or the community level. Biodiversity conservation is seen as a remedy to correct this trend by recognizing the "intrinsic worth of species, and of ecological barriers". According to Shiva and Moser (1995),

> A feminist and ecological perspective requires the encouragement of . . . convergences that will allow a post-reductionist paradigm of biology and politics to emerge. An important challenge for a post-reductionist approach is the need to evolve an ontologically coherent discourse for the domain of rights and responsibility. The controlled and unaccountable growth of the biotechnology industry is related to the ontological split between the domain of rights and the domain of responsibility which makes for an unrestrained and unaccountable system of rights. An ethical, ecological, feminist approach to biology, biodiversity and biotechnology can contribute to the evolution of a context of accountability and social control for the new technologies.

There is much that is arguable in these statements. Different groups and individuals see different responsibilities. As a member of the Recombinant DNA Advisory Committee of the U.S. National Institutes of Health, I have played a responsible role (and so did my fellow-members of the RAC) in monitoring and evaluating the ethical and safety factors which are likely to be environment-friendly. Biotechnology is here to stay because it is a part of the much larger progress of science and technology which has conferred many benefits to our society. A rational approach would involve both scientific excellence as well as a responsible attitude towards the environment, ecology and safety factors. To follow any other path would be turning the clock back and that is unthinkable.

Genetic engineering and redemptive technology

There are several aspects of genetic engineering which may be regarded as redemptive technology. Genetic engineering contributes to the understanding and conservation of genetic diversity of our plants and animals. It contributes to the future well-being of our society. Cole-Turner (1993) stated that the "preservation of genetic diversity is a redemptive intervention because it reverses an immediate consequence of unwise human action". One can clearly take issue with this statement. It is not clear to which "unwise" human action Cole-Turner is referring to. To say that genetic engineering is required solely to correct unwise human action is to deny the complexity of ecological forces, random evolutionary consequences, and the impact of the great number of surviving plant and animal species all of which have impacted adversely on occasion on our genetic future. To this list we should also add such periodic natural disasters as volcanic eruptions, floods, earthquakes, forest fires and other similar natural accidents all of which have contributed to the demise of some species of plant and animals. Surely we cannot blame "unwise" human action to explain the sudden extinction of dinosaurs.

Another example of redemption is as follows. Genetic engineering is useful for conferring disease resistance on agricultural plants, which, in turn, reduces dependency on fertilizers which cause environmental damage.

Redemptive intervention may also be seen by some in genetic screening techniques which contribute to a decision not to conceive a child at high risk or in selectively eliminating defective fetuses. Those who regard the life of a fetus as sacred may not find the latter practice acceptable. Similarly, prenatal diagnosis may occasionally lead to the treatment of a disease or, in some cases, it may result in abortion.

In addition to these above mentioned possibilities, one can visualize several other situations where redemptive action can restore normality. Human gene therapy (germline therapy) is one such remote possibility. For various technical and ethical reasons this method cannot be practiced at present. During this entire discussion, one is troubled by the flexibility of the meaning of the term "redemption". What seems to be clearly redemptive to one person would appear to be totally unacceptable to another, even though all such techniques tend to make the society a better place to live.

And what about racial or ethical equality? A recent case of a black mother in England giving birth to a white baby by means of the miracle of genetic engineering and *in vitro* fertilization may be viewed by some as being redemptive. Surely, it contributes to racial tolerance, if not equality? An appreciation of human diversity is surely redemptive because it contributes to peace and harmony in the world.

Following the same argument, one can visualize a whole world (surely, "a brave new world"!) in which redemption is achieved by adopting a program of positive eugenics. That is to say, instead of merely developing technologies to correct or prevent genetic defects in human populations, one can go beyond such methods to higher goals of improving existing qualities such as intelligence, musical abilities, and physical strength, etc. Furthermore, it may even be possible by applying redemptive technology to create whole new beings of "superior" quality or add on new organs with multiple functions which cannot be performed by the human body and mind as they are designed at present. Haldane (1923; also see Dronamraju, 1995) and Huxley (1932) have prophesied such possibilities. Individual beings who are specially suited to perform certain tasks in outer space, or under water, or on earth can be specially designed at will when biotechnology and genetic engineering are advanced to a higher level of sophistication.

Technology and creation

In the Hebrew scriptures, technology is often portrayed as evidence of God's activity. God was depicted as a gardener, or a builder, or a potter etc., but not as a natural object or a natural process. Gardening or agriculture is used as a metaphor for creation itself. Human beings are instructed to follow the divine work of creation and participate in the creation of natural order.

Cole-Turner (1993) presented arguments which connect God and technology including genetic engineering. He wrote: "If we are unable to imagine God as working though new technologies, we maintain a wall of separation between them and God . . . References to today's technologies are largely absent from liturgy, sermon, and theological literature". Perhaps the pace and complexity of genetic engineering has distanced itself from religious writers. On the other hand, it would be incorrect to say that God engages in genetic engineering.

Again, Cole-Turner (1993):

> Can we picture the creativity of God through the metaphor of our own abilities to alter genetic materials? An affirmative answer is consistent with the convictions of the Christian tradition through the centuries. It represents an important and decisive *expansion* of this traditional perspective, but it is not inconsistent with it.

Genetic engineering uses the natural process of recombination that has existed in nature since life began. Hence, it is argued that our use of recombination is a way to understand how God has been working in nature. It implies further that genetic engineering has the potential for being an extension of the work of God. Furthermore, "There is no limit to the possibilities of what God may yet create". Genetic engineering expands the purposes of God, or one might say that it is an extension of God's activity.

Cole-Turner's (1993) argument may be summed up as follows:

> God seeks genetic change as a proper means of creative and redemptive activity. God works through natural processes to achieve genetic change. The genetic

engineering in which God engages, and to which our involvement should be limited, is that which is consistent with the nature and purposes of God the Creator and Redeemer, who renews the whole creation in anticipation of a new creation.

Objection by religious leaders

Earlier, in May 1995, Rifkin joined several religious leaders, representing Protestants, Catholics, Jews, Muslims, Buddhists, and Hindus, to oppose the patenting of life forms, especially the patenting of animals and humans. They held a press conference on May 18, 1995, in Washington, D.C. Some of the key points presented at the press conference are :

> (a) genetic blueprints of life are the product of God and cannot be owned as "patented inventions" by any human being or institution.
> (b) by turning life into a patented invention, the government drains life of its intrinsic nature and value.
> (c) by redefining God's creations as "inventions," the government lays the legal and philosophical foundation for scientists and companies to assume the role of God.
> (d) some things in life are more important than "monopolizing" profits. Life is more than a commodity. The blueprints of God's creation should not be handed over to scientists and corporations just to insure greater profits.
> (Statement made available by the Foundation on Economic Trends, Washington, D.C., dated May 21, 1996.)

Civil rights and human rights?

Longtime biotechnology opponent, Jeremy Rifkin, and several well known leaders of the feminist movement, announced their opposition to the patenting of the BRCA1 breast cancer gene. The feminist leaders included Bette Friedan (USA), Gloria Steinem (USA), Bella Abzug (USA), Maude Barlow (Canada), Wangari Maathai (Kenya), Christine von Weizacker (Germany), and Vandana Shiva (India). The following is an excerpt from their statement:

> We oppose any attempt to patent the blueprints of our species. The effort to patent and commercially market the BRCA1 gene represents yet another assault on women–denying them control over the most intimate aspect of their being, their

bodies' genetic blueprints. Myriad did not invent the breast cancer gene–it merely discovered a gene that has long existed in the human gene pool. To claim it as an invention is as ridiculous as laying claim over the discovery of a chemical element like oxygen.... The corporate patenting of life is a new and insidious threat that needs to be challenged and defeated.

Rifkin further stated that his effort launched the "first genetic rights movement in history, which will loom as large as the civil rights and human rights movements". The International Coalition to Protect Human Genome, which was launched by Rifkin and others, is a collection of 250 women's, health, and social justice organizations from 68 countries (Brower, 1996). The president of Myriad Genetics, Peter Meldrum, reiterated that the BRCA1 test is useful in assessing risk and managing treatment choices; "those diagnosed with breast cancer have a 7-10 percent chance of recurrence, but women with a BRCA1 mutation have a 48 percent chance of developing a second chance" (Brower, 1996). Such women might choose to have a second, prophylactic mastectomy when first diagnosed. It is also obvious that it would be possible to monitor women with a strong family history of either breast or ovarian cancer who are detected to have the mutation. Frequent mammograms and pelvic ultrasound can be performed frequently. Women with a BRCA1 mutation have an 85 percent lifetime risk of breast cancer and a 50 percent chance of developing ovarian cancer.

The coalition spearheaded by Rifkin formally challenged Myriad's patent application by filing a legal petition with the U.S. Patent and Trademark Office. Furthermore, while not opposing genetic screening tests, Rifkin's group emphasized the need to protect privacy, confidentiality, and non-discrimination. However, other groups including the U.S. Biotechnology Industry Organization as well as various professional individuals have objected to Rifkin's attempts to link the patenting and privacy of discrimination, for instance in hiring and insurance protection–just to name two issues that are being experienced by those who are detected to possess the mutation and that need to be addressed with vigor.

Bibiliography

Adler, R.G. (1992), 'Genome Research: Fulfilling the public's expectations for knowledge and commercialization', *Science,* vol. 257, pp. 908-914.

Anderson, W.F. (1984), 'Prospects for human gene therapy', *Science,* vol. 226, pp. 401-409.

Adams, M.D., and Venter, J.C. (1996), 'Should non-peer-reviewed raw DNA sequence data release be forced on the scientific community?', *Science,* vol. 274, pp. 534-536.

Armstrong, J.A. (1993), 'Trends in global science and technology and what they mean for intellectual property systems', in *Global Dimensions of Intellectual Property Rights in Science and Technology,* edited by M.B. Wallerstein, M.E. Mogee, and R.A Schoen, Washington, DC: National Academy Press, pp. 192-207.

Balick, M.J., Elisabetsky, E., and Laird, S.A. (eds) (1987), *Medicinal Resources of the Tropical Forest.* New York: Stockton Press.

Bent, S.A., Schwaab, R.L., Conlin, D.G., and Jeffrey, D.D. (1987), *Intellectual Property Rights in Biotechnology Worldwide,* New York: Stockton Press.

Bentley, D.R. (1996), 'Genomic sequence information should be released immediately and freely in the public domain', *Science,* vol. 274, 533-534.

Bing, D.J. et al (1991) 'Potential of gene transfer among oilseed brassica and their weedy relatives', *Proc. 8th International rapeseed Congress, Saskatoon, Sask., Canada,* p. 1022.

Bozeman, B. and Crow, M (1991) 'Technology transfer from US Government and unversity R & D', *Science and Public Policy,* vol 11, pp. 231-236.

Brower, V. (1996) 'Rifkin marshals feminists against gene patents', *Nature Biotechnology,* vol. 14, pp. 814-815

Burch, K. (1995), 'Intellectual property rights and the culture of global liberalism', *Science Communication,* vol. 17, pp. 214-232.

Butler, D. (1995), 'Patent system gets vote of support from gene workers', *Nature,* vol 373, p. 376.

Caray, N.H. (1996), 'Why genes can be patented', *Nature,* vol. 379, p. 484.

Chernov, R. (1990), *The House of Morgan: An American banking dynasty and the rise of modern finance*, New York: Simon and Schuster.

Chomsky, N. (1994), *World Orders, Old and new*. New York: Columbia University Press.

Clegg, M.T., Giddings, L.V., Lewis. C.S., and Barton, J.H. (1993), 'Report of the International Consultation on Rice Biosafety in Southeast Asia' *World Bank Technical Paper, Biotechnology Series*, no. 1.

Cole-Turner, R. (1993), *The New Genesis: Theology and the Genetic Revolution*. Louisville, KY: Westminster John Knox.

Cole-Turner, R. (1995), 'Religion and gene patenting', *Science*, vol. 270, p. 52.

Collins, F.S. (1995), 'Positional cloning moves from perditional to traditional', *Nature Genetics*, vol. 9. pp. 347-350.

Dale, P.J. (1992), 'Spread of engineered genes to wild relatives', *Plant Physiol.*, vol. 100, p. 13.

Dale, P.J., McPartlan, H.C., Parkinson, R., MacKay, G.R., and Scheffler, J.A. (1992), 'Gene dispersal from transgenic crops by pollen', *Biogische Bundesanstalt fur Land*, Braunschweig, Germany, p. 73.

Davis, S.D. et al, *Plants in Danger*, Cambridge (UK): International Union for Conservation of Nature (IUCN).

Davison, F. (1996), 'Gene patenting', *Nature*, vol 279, p. 111.

De Zoeten, G.A. (1995), 'Risk assessment: do we let history repeat itself?', *Amer. Phytopathol. Soc Monogr.*, vol 81, p. 585.

Dickson, D. (1993), 'Mixed reaction greets new gene patents', *Nature*, vol. 363, p. 285.

Dickson, D. (1995), 'British MPs likely to oppose gene patents', *Nature*, vol. 373, p. 550.

Doremus, P.N. (1995), 'The externalization of domestic regulation. Intellectual property rights reform in a global era', *Science Communication*, vol. 17. pp. 137-162.

Dronamraju, K.R. (1989), *The Foundations of Human Genetics*, Springfield, Illinois: C.C. Thomas Inc.

Dronamraju, K.R. (ed) (1995), *Haldane's Daedalus Revisited*, Oxford: Oxford Univesity Press.

Eisenberg, R.S. (1994), 'Technology transfer and the genome project: Problems with patenting research tools', *Risk: Health, Safety, and Environment*, vol. 5, pp. 163-175.

Eisenberg, R.S. (1996), 'Intellectual property issues in genomics', *Bioinformatics*, vol. 14, pp. 1-6.

Evenson, R.E. (1993), 'Global intellectual property rights issues in perspective', *Global Dimensions of Intellectual Property Rights in Science and Technology*, edited by M.B. Wallerstein, M.E. Mogee, and R.A. Schoen, Washington DC, National Academy Press.

Frewer, L.J., Howard, C., and Shepherd, R. (1997), 'Public concerns in the United Kingdom about general and specific applications of genetic engineering: risk, benefit, and ethics', *Science, Technology, and Human Values*, vol. 22., pp. 99-124.

Fujimura, J.H. (1987), 'Constructing do-able problems in cancer research: Articulating alignment', *Social Studies of Science*, vol. 17, pp. 257-293.

Gadgil, M. (1995), 'The history of human impact on biodiversity', *Global Biodiversity Assessment*, edited by V.H. Heywood, Cambridge: Cambridge University Press, pp. 718-733.

Greaves, T. (1994), 'IPR: a current survey', *Intellectual Property Rights for indigenous Peoples: A Sourcebook*, edited by T. Greaves, Oklahoma City: Society for Applied Anthropology, pp. 1-16.

Haldane, J.B.S. (1923), *Daedalus, or Science and the Future*, London: Chatto & Windus.

Heywood, V.H. et al (eds) (1995), *Global Biodiversity Assessment*, Cambridge: Cambridge University Press.

Hoban, T.J. and Kendall, P.A. (1992), 'Consumer attitudes about the use of bitechnology in agriculture and food production' USDA-ARS Extensions Service, Chapell Hill: University of North Carolina.

Husain, A. (1991), 'Economic aspects of exploitation of medicinal plants', *The Conservation of Medicianl Plants* edited by O. Akerele, V. Heywood, and H. Synge, Cambridge: Cambridge University Press, pp. 125-140.

Huxley, A. (1932), *Brave New World.*, New York: Penguin.

Jayaraman, K.S. (1995), 'Patent changes in India clear path for US accord', *Nature*, vol. 373. p. 96.

Khalil, M. (1995), 'Biodiversity and the conservation of medicianl plants: Issues from the perspective of developing world', *Intellectual Property Rights and Biodiversity Conservation*, edited by T. Swanson, Cambridge: Cambridge University Press, pp. 232-253.

Kiley, T.D. (1992), 'Patents on random complementary DNA fragments?' *Science*, vol. 257, pp. 915-918.

King, S.R. (1996), 'Conservation and tropical medical plant research', *Medicinal Resource of the Tropical Forest: Biodiversity and its importance to human health*, edited by M.J. Balick, E. Elisabetsky, and S.A. Laird, New York: Columbia University Press, pp. 63-74.

Kuhn, T.S. (1962), *The Structure of Scientific Revolutions*, Chicago: The University of Chicago Press.

Kurth, J.R. (1979), 'Industrial and political change: a European perspective', *The New Authoritarianism in Latin America*, edited by D. Collier, Princeton: Princton University Press, pp. 319-362.

Lander, E.S. and Schork, N.J. (1994), 'Genetic dissection of complex traits', *Science*, vol. 265, pp. 2037-2048.

Lederberg, J. (1995), Foreword: J.B.S. Haldane's Daedalus–1923–70 years before and after. In: K.R. Dronamraju (ed), *Haldane's Daedalus Revisted*, Oxford: Oxford University Press.

Ledley, F.D. and Anderson W.F. (1996), 'Gene therapy for cardiovascular disease; an introduction', *Molecular Genetics and Gene Therapy of Cardiovascular Diseases*, edited by S. Mockrin, New York: M. Dekker, pp. 467-485.

Levin, M.A. and Israeli, E. (eds) (1996), 'Engineered Organisms in Environmental Settings: Biotechnological and Agricultural Applications', Boca Raton, FL: CRC Press.

McChesney, J.D. (1996), 'Biological diversity, chemical diversity, and the search for new pharmaceuticals', *Medical Resources of the Tropical Forest: Biodiversity and its importance to human health*, edited by M.J. Balick et al, New York: Columbia University Press, pp. 11-18.

McNeely, J.A. (1990), *Conserving the World's Biological Diversity*, Washington DC, IUCN, WRI, CI, WWF, and World Bank.

Mansfield, E. (1993), 'Unauthorized use of intellectual property: Effects of investment, technology transfer, and innovation', *Global Dimensions of Intellectual Property Rights in Science and Technology*, edited by M.B. Wallerstien, M.E. Mogee, and R.A Schoen, Washington DC, National Academy Press, pp. 107-145.

Marlier, E. (1992), 'Eurobarometer 35.1: opinions of Europeans on biotechnology in 1991', *Biotechnology in Public: A Review of recent research*, edited by J. Durant, London: Science Museum of the European Federation of Technology, pp. 52-108.

Mays, T.D., Mazan, K., Asebey, E. J., Boyd, M.R., and Cragg, G.M. (1996), 'Quid pro quo: Alternatives for equity and conservation', *Valuing Local Knowledge*, edited by S.B. Brush and D. Stabinsky, Washington DC, Island Press Inc. pp. 259-280.
Medawar, P. (1984), *The Limits of Science*, Oxford: Oxford University Press.
Michael, M. (1992), 'Lay discourses of science: science in general, science in particular and self', *Science, Technology, and Human Values*, vol 17, pp. 313-333.
Miller, H.I. (1996), 'Biotechnology and the UN: New Challenges, new failures', *Nature Biotechnology*, vol 14, pp. 831-834.
National Institutes of Health Technology Transfer Manual 1996, Office of Technology Transfer, NIH, US Public Health Service, Dept. of Health and Human Services, Bethesda, Maryland, USA.
Packer, K. and Webster, A. (1996) 'Patenting culture in science: Reinventing the scientific wheel of credibility', *Science, Technology, and Values*, vol. 21, pp. 427-453.
Palm, C.J. et al (1994) 'Quantification in soil of *Bacillus thuringiensis*', *Molec. Ecol.*, vol. 3, pp. 145.
Park, W.G. and Ginarte, J.C. (1996), 'Intellectual property rights in a North South economic context.', *Science Communication*, vol 17., pp. 379-389.
Pei-Gen, X. (1991) 'The Chinese Approach to medicinal plants–their utilization and conservation', *The Conservation of Medicinal Plants*, edited by O. Akerele et al, Cambridge: Cambridge University Press, pp. 79-124.
Posey, D.A. (1994), 'International agreement and intellectual property right protection for indigenous people' *Intellectual Property Rights for Indigenous Peoples: A Sourcebook*, edited by T. Greaves, Oklahoma City: Society for Applied Anthropology, pp. 223-251.
Rapaczynski, A. (1987), *Nature and Politics: Liberalism in the Philosophies of Hobbes, Locke, and Rousseau*, Ithaca, NY: Cornell University Press.
Reid, W.V. et al, (1996), 'Biodiversity prospecting', *Medicinal Resources of the Tropical Forest: Biodiversity and Its Importance to Human Health*, edited by M.J. Balick et al, New York: Columbia University Press, pp 146-173.
Sela, I. (1996), 'Engineered viruses in agriculture', *Engineered Organisms in Environmental Settings*, edited by M.A. Levin and E. Isreali, Boca Raton, FL: CRC Press, pp. 107-148.
Sharlin, H.I, (1989), 'Risk perception: Changing the terms of the debate', *Journals of Hazardous Materials*, vol. 21, pp. 261-272.

Shiva, V. et al (1991), *Biodiversity: Social and Ecological Perspectives*, London, UK and Atlantic Highlands, NJ: Zed books; Penang, Malaysia: World Rainforest Movement.

Shiva, V. and Moser, I. (eds) (1995), *Biopolitics: a feminist and ecological reader on biotechnology*, London and Atlantic Highlands, NJ: Zed books; Penang, Malaysia: Third World Network.

Sibley, K.D. (ed) (1994) *The Law and Strategy of Biotechnology Patents*, Boston: Butterworth-Heimann.

Soejarto, D.D. et al (1996), 'Plant explorations in Asia under the sponsorship of the National Cancer Institute', *Medicinal Resources of the Tropical Forest: Biodiversity and Its Importance to Human Health*, edited by M.J. Balick et al, New York: Columbia University Press, pp. 284-310.

Sparks, P. and Shepherd, R. (1997), 'The moral dimension of attitudes towards genetic engineering in food production' unpublished manuscript, quoted from Frewer et al.

Srinivasan, C.S. (1996), 'Current status and plant variety protection in India', *Agrobiodiversity and Farmer's Rights*, edited by M.S. Swaminathan, Delhi: Konark Publishers Pvt Ltd. pp. 77-82.

Swaminathan, M.S. (ed) (1991), *Farmer's Rights and Plant Genetic Resources, Recognition and Reward: A Dialogue*, Madras: Macmillan India Limited.

Swaminathan, M.S. (ed) (1996), *Agrobiodiversity and Farmer's Rights*, Delhi: Konark Publishers Pvt Ltd.

Swanson, T. (ed) (1995), *Intellectual Property Rights and Biodiversity Conservation*, Cambridge: Cambridge University Press.

Van Wijk, J. and Jaffe, J. (1996), 'Plant breeder's rights in Latin America: The effect on the transfer of foreign varieties', *Science Communication*, vol. 17, pp. 338-356.

Walden, I. (1995), 'Preserving biodiversity: the role of property rights', *Intellectual property rights and biodiversity conservation*, edited by T. Swanson, Cambridge: Cambridge University Press, pp. 176-198.

Zechendorf, B. (1994), 'What the public thinks about biotechnology', *Biotechnology*, vol. 12, pp. 870-875.

Index

ADA deficiency 123
Adler, R.G. 159
Anderson, W.F. 123-124, 159
animal varieties 28
Argentina 74-76
Armstrong, J.A. 146, 159
Asilomar conference 125

Bahamas 39
Bent, S.A. 27, 30, 159
Bethesda 125
Biogen 35
biological diversity 39, 84-89
Blaese, M.R. 123-124
Boyer, H. 26
Brave New World 123
Budapest Treaty 38-39
Burch, K. 148, 159
Bozeman, B. 35, 159

Calgene 34
cardiovascular disease 127
cell hybrids 29
Chakrabarty, A. 23-26
Chile 74-76
China 84
Chernov, R. 148, 160
Chomsky, N. 149-150, 160
CIMMYT 76
Clegg, M.T. 11, 160

Cohen, S. 26
Cole-Turner, R. 154-157, 160
Colombia 74-76
conservation 79-99
Convention on Biological Diversity (CBD) 39
Cornell University 32
CRADA 119-120
creation 156
Crow, M. 17, 160
cDNA sequences 101-114
cytokines 126

Daedalus 12
Dale, P.J. 55, 160
DNA 29
DNA probes 33
developing countries 130-139
Dronamraju, K.R. 12, 160

EC (European community) 37
Einstein, A. 20
erythropoietin 31
ethics 151-158
European Patent Convention (EPC)
Evenson, R.E. 2, 151, 161
Exxon Valdez 7

farmer's rights 67-68
Fujimura, J.H. 18, 161

Gadgil, M. 84
GATT 2, 66
"gene gun" 32
Genentech 32
genetic engineering 56-60
Geneva 37
Gilboa, E. 123
Ginarte, J.C. 129-131, 163
Global Biodiversity Convention 40

Haldane, J.B.S. 12, 15, 54, 161
Harvard mouse patent 34
Healy, B. 105
Huxley, A. 123, 156, 161
hybrid corn 34
Hybritech 33

InBio 87
India 72-76, 85-86
Indonesia 82-84
infrastructure 145
Intellectual Property Rights (IPR) 2, 3-5

Jayaraman, K.S. 161

Kendall, P.A. 53, 161
Kiley, T.D. 106-107, 162
Kurth, J.R. 148, 162

Lederberg, J. 12

McNeely, J.A. 82, 162
Madras (Chennai) 67
Mansfield, E. 1, 162
Mashelkar, R.A. 72

Mays, T.D. 94, 163
Medawar, P. 13, 163
medicinal plants 79-99
Meldrum, P. 158
Merck & Co. 87
Mexico 75-76
monoclonal antibodies 33
Mullis, K. 32
Myriad Genetics 158

NAFTA 75
National Cancer Institute (NCI) 79-99
Nepal 81
Newton, I. 20
New York University (NYU) 35
NGOs 75
National Institutes of Health (NIH) 101-114
NIH patent policy 115-121

Packer, K. 17, 163
Palm, C.J. 55, 163
Paris Union Convention 37-38
Park, W.G. 129-131, 163
Pasteur, L. 23
Patent Cooperation Treaty (PCT) 37
PCR 32
Pei-Gen, X. 84, 163
Plant Breeder's Rights (PBR) 41, 72-76
plant genetic resources 65-78
PHS Licensing Policy 116-117
Popper, K. 13
Pseudomonas aeruginosa 23
PTO Board 24, 76-77

Rao, C.R. 72
Rauvolfia serpentina 94
Recombinant DNA Advisory
 Committee (RAC) 9, 125
redemptive technology 154-158
Reid, W.V. 164
religion 13, 157
Rifkin, J. 157-158
Rio de Janeiro 39
risk 58-61, 164
RNA 29
Rosenberg, S. 123-124

Sela, I. 55, 164
Shiva, V. 61, 152-153, 157, 164
Sibley, K.D. 30, 164
Smith, P. 3
Soejarto, D.D. 82, 164
Stanford University 31
Swaminathan, M.S. 2, 10, 67-74, 164
Swanson, T. 164

Thailand 81
tomato 34

Tracy 62
transgenes 10, 35
transgenic dairy bull 61
TRIMS 66
TRIPS 66
Tumor Infiltrating Lymphocytes (TIL) 124

UNCED 39
UNEP 39
UPOV 43-44
Uruguay 74-76
Uruguay Round 65
U.S.-India S&T Pact 134-139
U.S. Congress 23
U.S. Supreme Court 23

viruses 56-58

Watson, J.D. 105
Webster 17
WIPO 37
WRI 66
WTO 147-148